Forward Motion

Sometimes the hardest part of moving forward is letting go...

by June R. Shrewsbury

Forward Motion

Copyright © 2016 June R. Shrewsbury

All rights reserved. No part of this book may be used or reproduced or transmitted in any form or by any means, electronic or mechanical, including photocopying, recording or by any information storage and retrieval system, without the written permission of the Publisher, except by a reviewer who may quote brief passages for a review.

For information regarding permission to reprint material from this book, please contact the publisher.

Limit of Liability/Disclaimer of Warranty. While the publisher and author have used their best efforts in preparing this book, they make no representations or warranties with respect to the accuracy or completeness of the contents of this book and specifically disclaim any implied warranties or merchantability or fitness for a particular purpose. No warrant may be created or extended by sales representatives or written sales materials. The advice and strategies contained herein may not be suitable for your situation. You should consult with a professional where appropriate. Neither the publisher nor the author shall be liable for any loss of profits or other commercial damages, including but not limited to, special, incidental, consequential or other damages.

The reader should be aware that Internet Web sites offered as resources and/or sources for further information may have changed or disappeared between the time this was written and when it is read.

ISBN 978-0-692-82431-3

Published by The ABCs of Everything, LLC
info@theabcsofeverything.com

Printed in the United States of America.

Table of Contents

Acknowledgments

Introduction

Chapter 1: Sixty to Zero in Sixty Seconds

Chapter 2: The Mourning After

Chapter 3: Denial ain't just a river in Egypt

Chapter 4: What Now?

Chapter 5: The Perils of Binge Watching

Chapter 6: A New Beginning

Chapter 7: How Did I Get Here?

Chapter 8: Finding a New Direction

Chapter 9: Visualize Your Ideal Outcome

Chapter 10: Take Action

Chapter 11: Build Your Support Network

Chapter 12: Overcoming Obstacles

Chapter 13: Make it Stick

Chapter 14: The Journey Continues

Forward Motion

Acknowledgments

This book would have not have been possible without the encouragement of my personal support system. It is with love and appreciation that I thank the following people:

To my husband who has been with me from the very beginning of this wonderful adventure, I couldn't have done it without your love and unwavering belief in me. You were always there when I needed you. You were supportive and encouraging and gave me the strength to reach for my dreams. You believed in me even when I didn't believe in myself. You gave me the greatest gift of all, our beautiful daughter. Our family is the inspiration for everything I do and I'm grateful every minute, of every day, you are in my life.

To my daughter, Samantha, you are the best part of what I have contributed to the world. You have grown to be a remarkable young woman and I am very proud of you. I appreciate the sacrifices you endured while I found my way in the world. My hope is that when you have children of your own, you feel the same joy as I have by having you in my life.

To my sisters, Susan and Theresa, without your love, encouragement and wonderful editorial input, this book would never have been completed. You believed the story I had to tell could be of benefit to others and helped me bring it to life. I would never have had the courage to do it alone. As we know, "the minds are severely linked" so this is as much your work as mine.

Forward Motion

Introduction

"Change is the only constant in life."
William Shakespeare

Change is one of the scariest words in the English language, or any other language. It ranks right up there with death, taxes, divorce and cancer. So why would I want to introduce you to such a word and what it meant to me? Because I have been there and because change is an inevitable part of life so you can't escape it. Some changes are small and insignificant and move you gradually along the path of your life. Some changes are so fundamental that you'll never experience life the same way again. I experienced the latter – my retirement after almost 28 years with the same company shook me to the core. Faced with reinventing myself and starting a new life, I was unprepared for the emotional roller coaster I was about to embark on. If you find yourself facing a similar situation, making a significant transition in your career or life, my story may provide new ideas and insights that could help you to understand, embrace and enjoy the experience.

I kept a journal in the early days of my

retirement. It was a way to process all the feelings I was experiencing. This book is in part a result of those musings. I was sure everyone would love to hear my thoughts on surviving a complete reinvention (*well maybe not*) but I decided to write the book anyway, if for no other reason than to look back on it in 10 or 20 years and remember who I used to be.

It wasn't until later it became apparent this book was part of the process. It was a way to memorialize the life I left behind and to plan for the life I was moving toward. An opportunity to share my experience in a way that could help others move forward with greater ease. Maybe even help them appreciate they were not alone in this experience and there are actions that can be taken to accelerate movement toward a more meaningful future. This was a cathartic journey for me. It helped me see how my life had evolved (*the good and the not so good*) and figure out what I wanted going forward.

Writing has always been a tool to help people make sense of the world. A way to capture who we are and reflect on what's happening to us. During a major life or career change, keeping a journal is not only a good way to process your feelings but to document the progress you're making. It can be hard to measure progress when you're in the moment, so having a journal to reflect back on can give you some distance and perspective to better appreciate the magnitude of the moment.

A journal can also be a great tool for thinking about what the future might hold. You can explore new ideas without risk. You can be very honest about what makes you happy or creates meaning for you without fear of having to share it with anyone else. You can "try out" what you want your life to be and how you feel about those choices. You can create a vision of your ideal life and take the actions that will lead you there.

All my life, I've turned to journaling when I needed to make sense of my world. It was in these words to myself I found my way through difficult situations. About ten years ago I was going through a rough spot and I was spending a lot of time journaling. But as often happens, life got busy. I set it aside and just forgot where I put it. About two moves and ten years later, I came across one of my journals. It was amazing that many of the "dreams" I had shared in it had come true for me. I had dreamt about a future that, at the time I wrote it, seemed impossible. But it was all the things I felt would make my life more peaceful and enjoyable. Just by putting these thoughts in my consciousness I was able to bring them to my reality. Not through overt action, but as I made decisions, my true desire was in my subconscious and guided me to make decisions that supported moving in that direction. In several chapters I've included actual excerpts from my past journals that reflect the processing that occurred. The dreams, the expectations, the highs and lows…the movement from a place of confusion to a place of understanding and contentment.

Throughout the book I write about some of the positions I held in my prior career. I don't mention the company name. You could substitute it for any large organization and the story would be the same. I was a senior leader in a large global corporation. What it took to reach that position is a similar experience regardless of the organization you chose (*and the topic for another book*). This story is not about my past life, but rather about what happened after I left that life and the process I went through to find a new future. A future more focused on who I wanted to be next.

It's been an interesting adventure, one filled with new awareness, new activities, new friends and colleagues, and in fact a very new me. It also included some difficult periods of self-doubt, depression and uncertainty. The process I used to get to here may be helpful if you are also at a reflective point in your life. I spent many years of my life gaining knowledge. Starting with a Bachelor of Science degree in civil engineering, then a Master of Business Administration and more recently adding a Graduate Certificate in executive and professional coaching. This academic learning paired with my life experience created the foundation for the story I want to relay. From my love of science and mathematics (*crazy I know*) to my deep appreciation of how to run a successful business, to my current fascination with helping people understand the depth of their own desires, I've created a process that works. My experience can help you find ways to reinvent yourself or to recover and move through a major transition in life. My intent is to guide you through a thoughtful process to discover who you are today and who you want to be tomorrow. Using the activities embedded in these chapters, you can discover the path to your ideal future.

Forward Motion

Chapter One

Sixty to Zero in Sixty Seconds

"Not until we are lost do we begin to understand ourselves."
Henry David Thoreau

It's amazing how fast things can change. One minute you're living your life, thinking this is the path you should be on when something happens and you find yourself in a brand new place. For me it was the decision to take early retirement. For others it could be a conscious choice or something forced upon them by circumstances beyond their control - a corporate restructuring, a health issue, a relocation, or just a growing feeling that the life you're living, is not the life you want. Regardless of how you got to this point, you are now in the throes of a major transition. It can be exhilarating, exciting, and terrifying all at the same time.

In these chapters you'll see there is a path forward, a process that can help you make sense of where you are, where you want to be and a way to find your path to a life that brings you meaning and joy. It's a process I know works because it worked for me. Using my life experiences and thought provoking coaching techniques I've helped myself and others make meaning of the significant changes in their lives.

The world I once lived in no longer exists for me. My days as a busy corporate executive are over. The complex life and the schedule I kept is foreign to me. My day began at 5:30 am, on the road by 6:30 am, and on a "short" day, home by 7:00 pm. Many weeks were spent in meetings in different cities during the day with evenings on an airplane heading to the next city. Weekends were used to catch up on sleep and prepare for the next week ahead. Vacations (*planned months in advance*) were an opportunity to fret over what I didn't get done before I left, sneaking a look at my email or making phone calls when my family was sleeping or otherwise engaged. I lived on a rigid schedule, balancing a million details to keep it all together.

When I was cleaning out my file cabinet last year, I found a file marked "relocation" that I created for our last move from Georgia to Texas. It made me laugh when I saw just how organized (*neurotic*) I was at that time in my life. In the file I found a detailed itinerary for each member of the family (*including the pets*!) outlining who was where, on what day, and where they would next be moved, complete with times, locations and modes of transportation. It reminded me of how complex my life had been and how stressful it was keeping all the balls in the air.

My new life is completely different. My purpose is now a true expression of who I am - no more alarm clocks and rushing to catch a plane, no more nights eating alone in a hotel room or stressing about the things I'm missing at home. I have found some balance. It's not always as exciting as it used to be, but I have a sense of contentment about my life that I never had before. Now when I go to "work" I'm helping someone else find the way to their happiness.

Many people who feel trapped in a situation don't realize they hold the key to their own freedom. If they took the first step, to explore what would bring them joy and fulfillment, they could be on the way to a happier life. This was the case for me. It wasn't until I stepped away from the life I had chosen that I was able to gain enough perspective to see how much I sacrificed in the name of "success". What I worked so hard to create had also robbed me of so many things, special moments with my family, my health and the joy of living life on my own terms.

When my daughter was in kindergarten I was working a project that required me to be in another city Monday through Thursday. I didn't realize how much it was affecting her until we went to her first open house. The teacher had asked the children to share their likes and dislikes. My daughter said the thing she disliked most was my job. When I asked her why, she said I wasn't there like the other mothers, I couldn't braid her hair before she went to school, I didn't take her to school or pick her up or work in the classroom. And even when I was able to do those things, it wasn't the norm, so it wasn't what she remembered.

As she grew up, my job continued to keep me away from my family at critical times. When she was a teenager, we were living in Georgia and I was moved to a new position in Texas. She was in the middle of her junior year of high school when I was relocated. I knew the move would be difficult, the timing was terrible, but I didn't feel I had the option to say no. It was so much worse than I imagined. I'd never seen my daughter so unhappy. It went on for months and it was heartbreaking. It was so difficult that my husband and I made one of the toughest decisions of our life - we decided that she and her dad should move back to Georgia without me so she could finish high school with her friends. We ended up living apart, me in Texas, them in Georgia, for almost two years. It was one of the worst periods of our lives and one regret I have never been able to let go. I missed my only childs' last year of high school. I wasn't there to take her picture when she put on her beautiful dress and headed out to the prom. Instead, I could only look at photos taken by someone else. I wasn't there

June R. Shrewsbury

when she was dealing with the normal transitions of early adulthood, her first serious boyfriend, her first job, leaving high school and preparing for college, and I left my husband to carry the load alone. (*If you were ever the parent of a teenage girl, you know what a heavy load that can be*). It was a tough time for the entire family and just a few of the many sacrifices we all made in the name of "success".

Early in my career I was identified as someone who had the "potential" to make it to a senior leadership level. It opened up a tremendous number of opportunities. I was offered additional training and development and many challenging assignments that demanded a lot of time away from home and frequent moves. At the time, I thought it was exactly what I wanted to do with my career. What I didn't appreciate was the impact it would have on me, and my family, and the sacrifices we all would have to make for me to get to the top of the organization. It wasn't until much later I realized this was not where I wanted to be or what was important to me.

Journal entry 8/30/2008: "It feels like I climbed the mountain, jumped through all the hoops, to reach the threshold of where I thought I wanted to go only to find it's not really what I want. When I think about what makes me happy, the answer is very simple. I love my family, I love my home and I love my privacy. I want a

17

different life going forward. I want to be healthy and energized. I want to spend time with the people I care about and I want to take more time for myself. Work is an important piece of my life but not the only one, I need to make it fit us, not the other way around."

It's worth mentioning that at the time I wrote this entry, I was an Executive Vice President responsible for a significant piece of a multi-billion-dollar business area. By all measures this was the type of position I had been working toward my entire career. However, finally there, I was stunned to realize that it wasn't making me happy. I wasn't where I was meant to be. It helped me understand that just because you're good as something, if it's not a true reflection of who you are, you need to question why you're doing it.

Looking back, I realize the situation had not been working for me for a long time. It wasn't until my doctor told me that my health was not good, and would continue to degrade unless I made a significant lifestyle change, that I began to contemplate a change. Much like the frog that doesn't feel the water heating up and fails to jump out of the boiling water before it's too late, my deteriorating health had simply crept up on me. I suffered from a chronic health issue which was exacerbated by living a life of constant stress, travel and not taking proper care of myself.

Continuing that lifestyle was not an option if I wanted both quality and quantity of life. My fear of losing my place in the world was so strong it prevented me from taking action until the stakes were life threatening. There were other telltale signs of discontentment that I managed to ignored as well – a lack of energy, a lack of interest in most things and a dullness that seemed to rob me of the joy of living. When this all became visible to me, I knew I had to find a new direction.

Journal Entry 11/8/13: "I want a longer, healthier life. I want to wake up feeling good not just going through the motions and pushing myself in spite of the pain. I want to be here when Samantha graduates, when she gets married and when she has her children. I want to be a healthy active grandmother who has the energy to keep up with my grandchildren. I want to use my time left on earth to create something enduring for my family."

Clarity of who you are and what makes you happy or brings you energy is critical to taking the first step. I've seen clients make remarkable changes in their lives, changes that allowed them to live the life they only imagined, by taking that first step.

One of my clients, a woman who was feeling trapped, a victim of her circumstances, realized that a better future was possible if she just let go of fear for a moment and visualized what a better future could look like. Her story was a familiar one. She had a job where she enjoyed working; a small company being acquired by a large corporation. When the change occurred, she found herself in a new environment that no longer aligned with who she was and what she loved about her work. Her energy came from the camaraderie the small group shared, the friendships she formed and doing work that spoke to her strengths.

After the company was acquired, she experienced a dramatic change in her job and work environment. Most of the people she worked with were reassigned to new positions or moved on, and without her prior consent, or input, she was placed in a series of different positions that did not align with her strengths. She began to feel less competent and less connected; things that had once made her job fulfilling. She realized the job was depleting her life energy and she needed to make a change but the fear of losing a paycheck was holding her back. With this clarity, she began the process of change that led to a new, fulfilling life doing things that brought her energy and happiness. She saw a path through to a new beginning. She envisioned another way to make money using her natural talents and abilities while working in an environment that gave her the social network and personal fulfillment she sought.

June R. Shrewsbury

As a result of the work we did together, she was able to see where she wanted her life to go. Where she wanted to live, who she wanted to be close to and most important, how she wanted to spend her time on meaningful and purposeful work. We crafted a plan of action that moved her from where she was to where she wanted to be in a very short time. Once she was clear about the future she desired, she created the actions and the support network to make it happen. We worked through strategies to overcome anticipated obstacles and even contingency plans for the inevitable setbacks. When I see her today, she's a different person. After years of chronic pain and weariness, she is now healthy and happy, living in close proximity to her children and grandchildren and pursuing a dream that will not only change her life for the better, but have a lasting impact on many others. Using the process outlined later she saw, and made, the necessary changes to create the life she dreamt about.

As you go through a major life or career change you must create a new story that taps into your core values and the person you are now, not the person you used to be. Altering your life can be a terrifying activity, full of fear and anxiety but it also can bring excitement along with new vitality and joy. The first step is the hardest, clarifying what it is you really want. What makes you happy? What brings you energy? Once you discover the answer to these questions, the process of change can begin. For me it was how, and with whom, did I want to spend my time. I wanted to use my talents to make a difference and find a purpose that went beyond a paycheck.

Whether change is precipitated by a job loss, a health issue or just disillusionment with your current situation; you may want to ask yourself this question, "How long am I going to wait to start living the life I only dream about?"

When I first started to think about leaving work I was exhausted. I was sick, stressed out and fed up with corporate life (*burn-out anyone?*). I had changed jobs four times in three years and moved a thousand miles away from my family (*again*) for 18 months. I was not satisfied with where I found myself, bottom line... I was not happy. After the worst annual physical of my life, I knew in my heart that if I kept working in this fashion I would be dead before I saw my first grandchild. That was a turning point for me. I made a tough decision and retired at the ripe old age of 55.

Being untethered for the first time in my life was both exhilarating and terrifying. One day I was the head of a large organization, leading thousands of people, responsible for hundreds of millions of dollars, never a free moment in a hectic schedule, hundreds of decisions to make every day and then, a minute later, I was retired with nothing but time in front of me. I had worked my entire adult life without a single break. The longest amount of unstructured time I'd ever had was about two weeks for a vacation and even then, work was calling me back at every opportunity. Now I had this unlimited expanse of time in front of me and wasn't quite sure what to do with myself.

Retirement was something I chose; it wasn't forced upon me. It was the right decision. But somehow that didn't prepare me for how I was going to feel. In the blink of an eye I went from being "somebody" to feeling like "nobody" in the eyes of the working world.

The transition was abrupt. Once I turned in my company phone and Blackberry I was cut off from the life I led for almost three decades. All my work colleagues were part of the past and I had to start all over again. I remember waking up the first day of my retirement with nothing on my calendar and thinking "now what"?

Most big changes start with a moment of terror. You have left something behind that is known and comfortable and now you're moving toward the unknown. It may be for the best, it may be expected or a deliberate choice, or a surprise and not welcome, but regardless of how you got there, it's uncharted territory and it takes time to understand and accept the changes. When an event occurs that shakes your very foundation it can feel as if you're a stranger in your own life.

A major transition often triggers a grief

response. The person you were is gone and the person you are destined to become has not yet emerged. You find yourself in limbo without a clear picture of where to go next. For almost three decades I defined myself by my job. Now I had no job. I couldn't help but wonder, "who am I now?"

Journal entry 1/30/14: "It's over...27 years and I'm finally free!!!! I turned in my phone, my computer, my secure id and my credit card. I just have to drop off my paperwork and badge and I'll never have to make the drive to work again! It still feels weird. I want to look for my Blackberry and check my messages. I wonder how long it will take before that urge goes away?"

    I believe the emotional trauma of a life altering change is similar for anyone that leaves a profession or situation they've been in for a long time. Especially if you enjoyed the work or the experience at one time and the people you interacted with during this time. Whether you choose it or it's forced upon you, it can be hard to move on. You miss the sense of purpose that the situation provided. You miss the relationships that you forged with like-minded people. You are no longer what had defined you in the world. Your identity, your calling card, the first thing you tell people when you meet them, is altered. You question whether you still have value, and if you do, what it is. My journey was unique but I suspect others in the grips of a major career or life change experience similar feelings. My transition began with a sense of great loss. I experienced what Elisabeth Kübler-Ross defines as "the five stages of grief" - denial, anger, bargaining, depression and acceptance. The process is different for everyone. Some people stay in one stage for a very long time or don't even experience some of the stages. The common thread is you have to go through a process of letting go to move forward to a new life. I recently caught an interview Norman Lear did with Oprah Winfrey. He said there are two little words in the English language that are so important - one is "over" and the other is "next". It can be hard to accept something is over but you can't move to your next life phase until you accept the last one is over. Deciding to walk away from the life I had was one of the most difficult decisions I ever made. It was the right decision, it was the right time, but that didn't change the fact that I was terrified. Harder still was coming to terms with the fact that it was *over* and now I had to figure out what was *next*. Regardless of the success you enjoyed, when it's over, it's over, and it's time to look forward, not back. There's a great song by Jason Mraz called "Living in the Moment", which became my anthem as I was creating my new life. In it he sings, "I can't walk through life facing backwards". It's a song about letting go of unproductive thoughts, forgiving yourself (*and others*) for past issues, things you can't change, and focusing on the current moment. You can, and should, bring with you the experience and talents from your past but you have to relate them to the person you're becoming not the person you used to be. The situation you left has ended and you have to accept it and begin again.

The different grief stages are responses to the myriad feelings you're experiencing. These feeling can last for minutes, hours or days. You move in and out of them throughout the process. You don't always begin or end individual stages in sequence. You may experience a wide range of emotions after such a significant change, from not caring to feeling angry or sad. You can go from feeling good, or even exhilarated, one minute to feeling devastated and lost in the next.

Early in my retirement an executive recruiter I had dealt with in the past contacted me. He wanted to know if I was interested in a CEO role that he was sourcing. I was ecstatic, I thought, "someone still thinks I have value, I can get back in the game". But in just a few minutes my thoughts went to what I had just left, and why, and how this would be the same thing all over again - the stress, the travel, the personal sacrifices and a lifestyle that would literally kill me. At moments like that, the enormity of what I walked away from was overwhelming. My biggest fear was I would never be as good as I once was. I wouldn't be able to duplicate the success I achieved in my prior career. I went from exhilaration to depression in the blink of an eye. And then, just when I'd begin to feel good about the choice I made, I'd hear about a former colleague who was moving up, taking on bigger responsibilities and it would remind me that I was standing still. It would plunge me back into self-doubt about what I'd done. My future was unclear and I didn't know if I would ever make a difference again. This cycle repeated for months.

How you react to a major life change is very personal and will be entirely different for every person.

Forward Motion

Chapter Two

The Mourning After

"Your life is what your thoughts make it."
Confucius

For the first few months after leaving work I read every book available about retirement. There must be several hundred out there, all focused on helping you "reimagine" and "reinvent" yourself. All of them spoke to me on some level but none of them could tell me how to make the most of the gift I'd been given - or worked very hard for, depending on how you look at it. The future was unclear and I was overwhelmed with the options in front of me and trying to decide which direction would bring me happiness and fulfillment.

Many people have done a good job of preparing for their financial life in retirement but haven't given much thought to what they will "do" with the rest of their lives. They have a list of pent-up activities they never had the time to do while they were working and that takes them through the first year, but there's nothing beyond that. Sitting on the beach sipping a drink is only entertaining for so long and then you need to find a purpose or reason to get up every day.

All the retirement books encourage you to "follow your passion" but I wasn't even sure what that meant for me. After defining myself a certain way for so long it wasn't clear who the real me was. Did I even have a passion? To me passion was a somewhat frightening word. It felt like losing control and if there was one thing I know about myself, it is that I like to be in control. As time went by, I came to see that finding my passion was about finding freedom. Freedom to experience life on my terms. Freedom to live a life of my own creation, with purpose and meaning aligned with my values.

Through the process I'll share with you, I was able to find my passion. I now know what brings me joy and purpose and how I want to live my life but it took time and a lot of self-reflection to reach that point. I had to learn to let go of what was comfortable and be willing to learn new things. After years of being an expert in my field, I had to be willing to start over and be vulnerable and inexperienced. I had to become comfortable with not being the one with all the answers and having to ask for help while experiencing the frustration of starting all over.

June R. Shrewsbury

    When I decided to become a coach I knew it entailed learning new skills. In my past life I was the one that people came to for answers. In coaching it's all about helping the client find the answers that are inside them. The very worst thing you can do is to try to provide answers for them. It was a struggle to just listen to a client and suspend my own thoughts (*and judgments*) and hear the answers the client was communicating. My immediate inclination was to jump in and tell them what I thought they should do. It took a lot of patience and practice to learn to trust the client could find the solution that fit them and not try to superimpose my own life filters on what they knew was the best course for them. It wasn't an easy skill to learn but it was important enough to me in achieving my desired outcome that I was willing to do the work necessary to master it. At times I questioned if it was even possible for me to make so dramatic a change. Working with my own coach to develop my coaching techniques helped me overcome my biases. By practicing over and over again with a lot of clients, I began to gain confidence that I could be an effective coach. To this day it's still something I think about going into each coaching session.

    My passion now is coaching others as they too experience career and life transitions. In coaching others through life altering change, this question of passion is a common theme. Many people start coaching by asking, "Where do I start?" "How do I find my "passion"?" "How do I know what brings me real joy?" "How do I make it happen while I'm living the life I have now?" They know where they are is not making them happy, but they don't know how to take the first step that will lead them to a better place. My focus is on helping them discover and harness their unique talents to live a more meaningful life.

I can relate with new clients because I too was unprepared for figuring out a different path. Like many people, I tended to live in the future. There is an implied "deferred life" concept in our society, we work hard for many years so that we can retire well at some distant point in the future. We pin all our hopes and dreams on some place in the future where we are happy and fulfilled without a care in the world. So we work hard and sacrifice the present to get there. Unfortunately, when you get there you realize you can't go back and recapture the moments you missed, or the relationships you lost or the health you compromised. I asked myself, "When is it time to live the life that brings me joy?"

Journal entry 8/2/2009: "Today my horoscope said..."Focusing too much on the future keeps you from appreciating where you are now". I guess I need to keep in mind that today is a good day as well. I have so much to be grateful for everyday and sometimes I take it for granted. The world around us seems to be going out of control yet we are doing well. We have a great life – nice home, enough of everything we need, a loving family..."

It was a bit of joke in our family that I would plan our vacations for the next year long before the current year was over. With only a limited number of vacation days I wanted to make sure we made the most of them. I'm convinced I was the only executive in my company that used every vacation day earned every year without fail (*this should have been my first clue I was looking for a way out*). I was always looking to the future to find happiness. When the present was too much to bear, I'd escape to the future.

When considering what would bring me happiness I started with an examination of how I defined success. For many years that was a number. How much money did I have? Did I have the external artifacts that told the world I had arrived? It also included a need for recognition and to feel valued by the external world. Was I a leader in my field? Was I sought out for advice? Over time I came to realize that success was so much more.

Success for me now is living an authentic life – not the *fantasy* of a great life, but a great life. A life that allows me to do things that are of value to the world but to do them on my terms. To be present in the moment, happy now, not longing for future happiness. To have meaningful relationships and help others reach for their dreams and share in their success.

Defining success according to your own values allows you to live a more authentic life. My initial definition of success was too limiting. It was too dependent on the opinion of others and external validation. I now realize the only opinion that really matters is my own. That may sound egotistical but it's not meant to be. The point is I'm the only person who can live my life. I'm the only person who knows what brings me joy and satisfaction and it's up to me to decide every day what is the best way to spend that day. If I'm living my core values, each day can be meaningful and purposeful.

I found my way to acceptance by looking at the world in a different way. I wish I could say this was an immediate insight, but it was not. I still had to go through the grieving process and let go of the person I was to see the person I could be. You can take comfort in knowing that with time, you will find new ways, new things, and even new people to be with. You'll discover a world you never knew existed.

Acceptance is all about acknowledging what has changed and learning to embrace that change. Over time you begin to find peace with what happened and you can envision a new and better life.

Chapter Three

Denial ain't just a river in Egypt

"The secret of change is to focus all your energy, not on fighting the old, but on building the new."
Socrates

Denial starts with questioning yourself - Did that just happen? Is it too late to go back and make a different decision? What was I thinking?!!

In the early days of retirement, I found myself longing for the "good old days" when I had a clear sense of purpose and a place to go every day. I struggled to find meaningful ideas to replace my work.

Retirement started with a plan and several lofty goals. I'd exercise every day, follow a healthy diet, mediate and do yoga to enrich my soul, organize my closets and my 30 years of photographs, learn to dance and cook and paint and sew... and a million other things I always thought looked creative and fun. Being an overachiever, I made a comprehensive list of all these things and started down the list. I was terrified of having "unstructured" time and having to face the fact my life no longer had a clear purpose.

    I discovered that not all of those things were as interesting as I hoped they would be. Alas, my closet is still not organized. It turns out it's just as tedious to do when you have the time as when you don't. I did enjoy looking at my life in photographs and walking down memory lane (*for a day or two*) but when it came to figuring out what to do with them, they also fell into the not very interesting pile.

    I discovered I was pretty good at sewing and I enjoyed making something with my hands. But after I made too many pillows, Christmas stockings and table runners, I was ready to move on. I felt the same about cooking. I enjoyed trying out new recipes. I signed up for cooking lessons and had fun with it… for a while. Then I realized it was conflicting with my "healthy eating" to some degree because I tended to prefer the sweet, buttery recipes to the vegetarian and healthy dishes. So this too went the way of the sewing.

    Next I threw myself into several projects that were interesting and more important, time consuming. For my mother's 80th birthday I created a collage of photos of all her descendants. It put me back in touch with many family members and was a nice tribute to her life. I discovered the miracle of Photoshop and had a great time making old pictures look better (*mostly pictures of myself*). I explored my creative side but I found this too was not enough.

June R. Shrewsbury

My daughter gave me the favor of getting engaged just after I retired. Her wedding became another project to immerse myself in with lots of busy work. I spent hours agonizing over every detail. I created a different spreadsheet for every major aspect; invitations, hotel reservations, wedding timelines, you name it, I had a spreadsheet for it. When we couldn't find the exact table runner she wanted, I volunteered to make them (*I now had the time and sewing skills as you know*). We met with photographers and DJs, listened to bands, attended wedding conventions, enjoyed cake and catering tastings and shopping, lots of shopping, for her wedding dress, for all the other outfits we'd need for all the wedding events, and for everything from bubbles to hanging teardrop lights for the trees. I enjoyed this time with my daughter helping her plan her wedding; it was another distraction from thinking about where my life was headed. When the wedding was over I was back to looking for my next project.

So just to make sure every moment was consumed, we built a vacation home in another city. We had planned to have the architect be the Project Manager. Then I decided I could do it better and of course… I now had the time to do it. As with the wedding, the first order of business was to create a project plan with detailed instructions for the construction and decorating of the cottage. Having spent the better part of my career as a program manager this was my comfort zone. I gave it the same level of intensity I gave my work projects - much to my contractors' dismay. What started out as a single story 1200 square-foot cottage evolved into a two-story 2400 square-foot house. As the construction got under way I had so many "great" ideas that needed to be incorporated. It started with a change in the height of the ceilings and ended with the addition of a whole new floor requiring a new staircase and rearrangement of the original floor plan to accommodate it. The roof had been placed on the house before I decided to take advantage of the attic space so we had to cut into the new roof just days after it was completed to add windows. Then I started changing the details - light fixtures, sinks, countertop, tile, etc. One again, there was a spreadsheet for every room with every detail outlined - floor covering, paint color, light fixtures, etc., down to the part number, for the contractor to follow. In the end, I suspect he didn't use any of it. He was a very experienced contractor and knew how to track his own work, but it made me feel better to have control in a spreadsheet.   I felt I had control over my life again, I was making plans and executing them. I continued to struggle with giving up my persona of the past and adopting a different attitude toward life. This was the "denial" phase for me. If I just kept very busy, nothing would change. I'd still be the busy executive I always was.

June R. Shrewsbury

My husband and I (*yes, he did exist during all this*) decided we needed to make up for all the times we didn't go the places we wanted to because of work demands. We took lots of short trips to visit family and friends (*and a few too many to the casino*) and enjoyed the spontaneity of it all. The best part was when we got away I could be present in the moment; there was no "work" in the background waiting to call me back. The insane thing was I missed it. My Blackberry had been a part of me, something I was never without, and I found myself pining for it at times. There was a sense of being needed that evaporated along with my job. We all know that we're "replaceable" but when it happens, it's difficult to accept that someone else is doing the job you did for so long and your input is no longer required. Every trip we took was enjoyable, but is still felt like a way to kill time until I figured out what was next. I felt a void in my life and was not quite sure how to fill it.

Forward Motion

Chapter Four

What now?

"Do not dwell in the past, do not dream of the future, concentrate the mind on the present moment."

Buddha

When you begin to accept the reality of what has happened and question yourself about what's next, you're taking the first steps toward a new beginning.

Journal Entry 2/25/14: "I need to think about what I really want in the future. Do I want to work and if so at what? I don't think sitting around the house is a good idea. I do need time to "reset" but that can't be forever. I need to answer some very basic questions about what I want out of the life ahead of me. What is my passion?? What will engage me and bring me joy?"

After my denial period, I hit the "anger and bargaining" phase about the same time. I was angry at myself for not being able to let go of my past and embrace what might come. I would wake up thinking "Why can't I just be thankful for this great opportunity and relax and enjoy the moment?" I vacillated between regret and happiness - then the bargaining started. Could I just be comfortable with my new status and enjoy the freedom? Should I go back to work? If so, what type of work would give me the lifestyle I wanted but still fill the void that my past job had left? How much time did I want to spend with my family? Was it too much now? Was I kidding myself all those years when I thought I was missing out on something while I was at work? Did I just make the biggest mistake of my life?!! Bargaining gave me a glimpse into all the options I might have in front of me. It was a preview of the different places I could take my life. Bargaining allowed me to begin to restore order to my life and move forward.

Journal Entry 4/8/14: "This morning I'm meeting Samantha in Trinity Park so we can walk the 5k route we did last weekend. This is what retirement is all about. I can do what I want, when I want, I can spend time with Samantha and Tom and just "stop and smell the roses". I've been meditating and trying to shift my thinking to a calmer, more serene place. I think it's starting to take hold. The changes I made will give me a *great chance for a longer and healthier life. I'm so grateful that I was able to retire early. This is just the beginning of a very bright future."*

My financial advisor once told me that he saw many people who "failed" at retirement. Not financially, but emotionally, because they just couldn't find a new purpose as meaningful as the life they left. I didn't want to be one of those people. I wanted to find the right job or situation that would give me the things I was missing about work and at the same time allow me to enjoy my new found freedoms.

Some days I woke energized and felt like this was the greatest experience of my life. I had nothing but new opportunities in front of me. Other days I woke feeling like I made a huge mistake. If I had just hung in there I could have been a successful executive moving up the corporate ladder once again. On those days, my husband reminded me that if I had continued, I would most likely be dead by now....so not moving so fast.

What I wanted to do was fill every minute with "something". I wanted to feel as worthwhile in retirement as when I was working. I spent a lot of time thinking about what I should do with all this time on my hands.

Journal excerpt 5/10/14: "I'm starting to develop a routine for my days. I keep dreaming about work. I guess I'm working through the process of letting go of that person I was. It's a bit unsettling at times. I panic when I think about what I walked away from. I know in my heart it was the right decision but it still feels strange not to be working, not to have a specific identity to align with. I feel like I'm not a very interesting person any more. Which is sort of funny considering I was never able to talk about what I did. I can speak much more freely now and discuss things that interest me. Samantha and I were talking yesterday about my idea to write a book about transitioning to retirement. I'm coming to the realization that it's probably very different for everyone based on how much you used your professional life to define you."

For my entire adult life, I had defined myself by the work I did. Learning to let go of that was going to take time and effort. The good news was, I had the time and was willing to put in the effort to create a new life that brought me satisfaction and a sense of purpose.

Chapter Five

The Perils of Binge Watching

"Most people are as happy as they make their minds up to be."

Abraham Lincoln

    Depression is nature's way of protecting us by shutting down the nervous system so we can adapt to something we feel we just can't handle at the moment. But depression has elements that can be helpful as well. It slows us down and allows us time to understand the changes we're experiencing. It helps us begin the process of rebuilding ourselves.

    The hardest part of the grieving process is when you hit "depression". I knew I had arrived at it when I started binge watching old NCIS episodes. I could sit in front of the TV for hours on end. I didn't want to go out, I didn't want to talk to anyone, I just wanted to pass time. It started with a minor injury; a herniated disc in my upper back. It wasn't life threatening or anything serious but it was painful and required several months of physical therapy. For about two months I wasn't able to do much, so I spent a lot of time in a semi-reclined position with ice packs on my back. I used that as an excuse to hide out. However, it was also a time of deep reflection for me.

I was mourning the loss of my prior self and struggling with who I was to become. For so many years I knew what was expected of me. I knew how to play the game. I was confident in my ability to be the person I needed to be to get the job done. And then in a nanosecond, it was all gone. I had to re-create myself in a new image. I needed to define a new path and I didn't have a clue as to where to start.

I missed the personal interactions. I missed the friendships I had developed. After I left work I lost contact with colleagues I had felt so close to all those years. I could no longer just pick up the phone and chat about what was happening in the business. It felt like I had put myself in isolation. I know I could have initiated contact with my prior colleagues but it felt wrong to bother "busy" people when I believed I had nothing to contribute. I remembered the fun part of my work and forgot about the rest (*selective memory is very prevalent in this stage*).

I had so many interesting and fun adventures at work, traveling in foreign countries, experiencing the wonder of being in a new place, working with a group of people that shared a common bond. On a trip in Argentina, a group of us had driven from Cordova to Villa Mercedes. It was a long car trip and there were five of us traveling together. One was a translator because none of the rest of the team spoke Spanish. We thought we were lost and stopped to get directions from one of the locals in a small town along the way. After a very lengthy exchange (almost a full minute) between the translator and the local, we asked her to tell us what he said; "he said go straight". That became the standard response to every question for the rest of the trip. We laughed all the way to our final destination. Every trip produced these kinds of inside jokes and moments of fun between the meetings, shared meals in exotic places, harrowing car trips, entertaining shopping encounters and always a sense of belonging... The parts of the job I missed.

What I didn't miss was the inordinate amount of time I spent at airports. I learned that you should take the earliest flight of the day (*least potential for delays caused elsewhere in the system*). Friday evening out of National in DC is the worst time to fly, and if you can avoid the summer months entirely (*too many inexperienced travelers and unaccompanied minors slow down the process*) it's best for all. My schedule involved traveling to two or more cities in a week, working all day and then flying all night to the next destination. Always getting into a city late, checking into a hotel for a very brief amount of sleep before I had to get up, pack, work all day and then head to the next location. Some people see glamour in traveling, but that was not my experience. More often, it was crowded airport lines, bad fast food, noisy hotel rooms, and a sense that I was missing out on my life at home with my family.

As with other things in life, you tend to remember the past with "rose colored glasses". No one wants to remember the pain, only the good things and I learned that savoring the past too much can be unhealthy. It led to many sleepless nights and the realization that if I couldn't let go, I couldn't move forward.

Depression has also been characterized as "anger turned inward". You're at a point where you might be angry with yourself for not having made different decisions, or for not having greater insight into where you might go next. You want to move forward but you just can't see the place you want go. Your frustration causes you to just shut down and block out the world. I know that I was not easy to live with during this phase. My natural optimism was at an all-time low and I was not fun to be around. I thought the best thing for everyone was for me to isolate myself (*my husband often agreed*). For some this stage may be something that requires more than just self-reflection. But for me, after a few agonizing months I decided this is not where I wanted to spend any more time. I began to focus on the things in my life that I was grateful for and how I could use them to make a new life that was better aligned with my true self. My journal became the place I was able to reflect on who I was now, process those feelings of loss, and take the initial steps toward defining what the future looked like for me. That process helped me to move forward. *(That, and my new rule that I was not allowed to turn on the TV until after 6:00 pm).*

Forward Motion

Chapter Six

A New Beginning

"What we think, we become."
Buddha

After what seemed like a very long time I reached a point of acceptance; I was now in a new phase of life. I was no longer a corporate executive. I was "retired" and soon to be defining a new career for myself. There was no going back. This stage is all about accepting your new situation. It's understanding your new "normal" and shaping it to be the best it can be. This is where reinvention starts. You let go of who you used to be and begin to create who you want to be.

It started with a phone call from my sister. It was 3:00 in the afternoon and she asked me what I was doing (*watching NCIS of course*). She told me, in a firm, but kind way (*well maybe not so kind*) to turn off the TV, get off the couch and figure out how to move forward. I knew she was right; I needed to consider what the next 30 years were going to look like for me. It was time to move on to the rest of my life. This was the beginning of a great adventure for me.

When I retired I intended to take a full year off before pursuing anything new. I wanted to get to a point of knowing who I was without work. What did I like and dislike, who was I when there was no one around to tell me who I should be? It was a bit frightening to confront my real self after all the years of being an extension of the job I held.

I discovered while my values were much the same, how I felt about the world had changed in a significant way. I no longer needed the external validation I once thought was so important. Don't get me wrong, we all love "the applause", but it was no longer important to my future. I wasn't looking for the next promotion or trying to impress anyone. Everything I did from this point forward was what I *wanted* to do and nothing I *had* to do. I could live my life on my own terms.

Many of us are so caught up in who we should be, we forget who we are. We all seek the same things, approval, validation, love and belonging. We accept the life roles that we believe will bring those things to us. Yet we don't have to be constrained by those roles. One of my greatest insights was that my family and the other important people in my life didn't care what I did for a living. They loved me for the person I was, the values I held and the relationships we shared. What I did for a living had nothing to do with it.

This was a huge epiphany for me. It freed me from worrying about what I did and allowed me to focus on who I was and how I wanted to experience the rest of my life. I felt free to create any life I chose.

Journal Entry 7/14/14: "I realize I feel guilty telling people how happy I am now that I don't have to work anymore. I also feel guilty that I'm in such a great place and so many people I love are not. I know that is an unproductive thought. We all make choices in our lives that define the outcome. I worked very hard, sacrificed my health, impacted my personal relationships and missed a lot of family milestones to get to where I am today. Now I'm able to reap the rewards so I will not feel guilty any more. I will feel gratitude and be happy in the knowledge that from this point forward I can have a more balanced, peaceful life surrounded by the people I love. This is what I was working for all along but now that it's here, it's better than I even imagined. I love the freedom to do whatever I want. I don't have to be careful about what I say or do and I can change my plans when it suits me. I know that next year I'll work again. But it will now be on my terms, doing something that interests me and allows me to work at the pace I choose and in the manner I choose. I'm not sure where we will be living or how much time I will want to dedicate to *work but it will be my decision. I think this is what retirement is all about - Gaining freedom to do what you really want to do."*

After I'd been retired about a year, my daughter sent me a photograph that was taken just before I retired. It was amazing that not only had I gone through an emotional transformation, I also had gone through a physical transformation. It wasn't just my hair style that was different, or that I'd lost a few pounds or changed my clothing style; what was different was there was the lack of tension in my face and in my body language. You could see the difference; the sense of peace and contentment I felt was reflected in my appearance. People I hadn't seen for a long time didn't recognize me. I went to see my former assistant. We hadn't met in at least three years. When I walked into her office she said she wouldn't have recognized me if she passed me on the street. The physical changes reflected the internal changes I had made.

Journal Entry 11/01/14: "Another month has passed and I can't believe I've been retired for 9 months now. I decided to go back to school and get a certificate in executive coaching. I'll be in school for the next year but then I can start a consulting business for the future. It will give me the flexibility to work as much or as little as

June R. Shrewsbury

I want. Just enough to keep my mind active but not too much to put me on a bad path again with my health. I'm excited about starting something new after all these years. I've always enjoyed school and learning but never really had the time to pursue it. I think it will be a great way to meet some new people in the area as well. When I got the letter from UTD I experienced a moment of panic. Can I go back to school at 55? Then I thought...why not? I still have 20 - 30 good years ahead of me and I'm not going to spend them watching TV. I may find something else I like while I'm in school. This could be the first step to my "encore career". I'm excited to try something new."

Forward Motion

Chapter Seven

How did I get here??

"If you do not change direction, you may end up where you are heading."
Lao Tzu

Throughout my career, I traveled around the world, I did what was expected of me, and by all external measures had a successful career. I earned my way into the "million-mile" club with one airline and almost did with another before I stopped my business travel. However, the toll it took was significant.

I got to this place by following a strict work ethic - or as my daughter called it "being a workaholic" (*we laughed about the fact that while it was technically an addiction, it was at least a socially acceptable one*).

My work was everything you would think makes a great career. I worked with exceptional, intelligent people on interesting and meaningful projects. I believed every day (*and still do*) that the work we did made the world a safer place. I was well compensated for my work and always felt appreciated. So why did I get so disillusioned with it all? That's a question I still can't answer. I'm sure the long hours and stressful business environment contributed to it. I think my health issues affected my overall emotional state in a negative way and I think I was just exhausted, mentally and physically, and needed a few months of sleep.

It was only as a result of my coaching education that I discovered my basic personality style was at odds with the work I was doing. Every day when I went to work I had to adapt and adjust my true self to do the job. Even though I was able to adapt, every day the work depleted my energy and I didn't do enough outside of work to replenish it. The cumulative effect was a bad case of "burn out" and more health issues than a person my age should have.

I was a female leader in a male dominated business at a time when women were just beginning to make strides in the business world. When I entered my first leadership position women were still an anomaly in management. It was both an advantage and disadvantage to be a woman in the industry at that time. Women were very visible, when you did good work (*or bad*). There were still a lot of misconceptions about how effective we could be in senior executive roles. I saw myself as a trailblazer for the women who followed me. It was responsibility I took to heart and it increased the pressure I put on myself to perform. I felt the need to work harder than ever to prove I was capable of doing the job and entitled to be where I was. This had a huge impact on my stress level. I was always trying to do just a little more, check my work one more time, be a perfectionist, so no one would think I wasn't as competent as my male peers. I lived in a near constant state of stress. *(I could have been the poster child for the negative effects of stress on the human body).*

I led big, complex programs and businesses and enjoyed a very colorful life for many years. I traveled all over the world and met interesting people. I toured the Pyramids in Egypt and dined at the best restaurants in the world, I attended trade shows in Paris, London, Singapore and Greece. I interacted with ambassadors, senior US government officials and even royalty. It was an exciting career and I was grateful for the opportunities I was given. However, it also meant I was always working and traveling and my life was usually out of balance.

I used to think I had achieved work/life balance by compartmentalizing my life. I would say, "I can have it all, I just can't have it all at the same time." I believed it was just a matter of good time management. I could be present in the place I occupied at the moment, work or home or with friends or family, and the other part of my life would just cease to exist for a time. For many years that strategy worked for me. But the long-term impact of living that way was an inability to just relax and replenish. The "job" meant I had to be accessible 24/7 and never able to break away from the work. Most holidays and vacations were interrupted at some point by a phone call or urgent meeting. Even when this wasn't the case, my mind was always on the work that needed to be done when I got back. When I was at work, all the things I was missing at home were in the back of my mind. The stress just continued to build.

In the end, I realized no matter where I was or what I was doing it was still just a job. It wasn't the real me. I enjoyed the people but I hated the travel, staying in hotels (*however nice they may be*) eating at restaurants for every meal and not seeing my husband and daughter for weeks on end. I can remember many times sitting in a hotel room praying that I would just wake up in the morning. My greatest fear was that I would die on the road in a city where I knew no one and it would take a day or two for them to find me. It was terrifying and I knew at some level I couldn't keep up this lifestyle.

I never liked being away from home but that was the job I signed up for. When you're trying to work your way up the corporate ladder it's hard to say no to any assignment. It's easier to deal with the fallout in your personal life and convince yourself that you are "doing it for them" when in reality you are doing it for you, for your ego and your advancement. That's a tough realization but all too true.

June R. Shrewsbury

One of my favorite lines is from Frank Sinatra's song *My Way*, "Regrets I have a few…but then again too few to mention". I think that sums it up well. If I had the chance to do it all again I might do a few things different, but not many. I learned so much with the experiences I had. I'm grateful for the many opportunities and the wonderful people I had the pleasure to know. That unique set of experiences created who I am today, the good and the bad, and allowed me to see my own potential. It gave me confidence that I could do anything I put my mind to, that I could overcome any obstacle and survive any crisis. It also taught me what's possible when you're willing to take risks and say yes to new opportunities. I took every opportunity offered to me even if it wasn't perfect. I took the hard jobs requiring long hours and total commitment but offered the greatest financial and professional rewards. In the end, I experienced both the benefits and the impact of those choices. I left the company a senior executive with a comfortable financial future ahead of me but with some health challenges that will always be with me.

When I announced my retirement, I received dozens of notes from people I had worked with in the past. Most were notes of gratitude for something I had said or done the made life a bit easier or more meaningful to them. Some were from people that I hadn't seen or spoken to for years. Some were from people I never knew but had worked in an organization with me and they just wanted to thank me for making it a better place to work. Many were just a simple message that said, "You made a difference in my life". As a leader, my goal was always to help those around me make the most of their experience. I felt if they were happy and engaged in their work they would be more productive and the business would thrive.

    That was the part of my job I will always miss. The work was interesting but it was the people that made me want to be there and what I missed most when I retired. It was also these thoughts that led me to find my passion. When I considered what made me happy I realized it was helping other people find their place in the world. I took this thought and created a vision of a future life allowing me to do it all the time.

    After I retired I often had dreams about work. I dreamt about people I hadn't seen in years and I miss them still. Probably the hardest part of retirement is letting go of your "work friends" and finding new friends that fit with the new you. That's something else the retirement books don't talk about. There's considerable discussion on financial preparedness and tricks to extend your money. Lots of advice is offered on how to spend your time pursuing charitable work, and even finding your "encore career" but very little on the emotional impact changing your life can have on you and those around you.

June R. Shrewsbury

Journal Entry 8/14/14: "I'm feeling very unsettled again this week. More crazy dreams about prior work people. I'm not sure when that stops. I know in my heart that retiring was the right decision and probably saved my life but I'm still mourning my career a bit. I had a lot of stress but I also had a lot of fun. My decisions made a difference and now I don't have that same impact. I know those closest to me appreciate me being here but I'm not having a great impact anywhere else. I think that's the hardest part. I feel useless and bored sometimes. I think I don't have much time left on the planet so I should be doing more. But I don't want to do something because I think I "should" I want to do it because I "want" to do it. But what do I want to do?? That's a tough question. I've been given this great opportunity to do anything I want but I'm not sure how to decide what that is. It's almost like I'm starting my life all over again. Exciting but scary at the same time. Do I launch a new career? Do I settle into life as a retired person? Do I do something in between? All questions I have no idea how to answer at this moment in time."

Nine months into my retirement (*and 12 seasons of NCIS*) I knew I had to find a new path for myself. I had caught up on my sleep. I was feeling healthy, both physically and mentally, and I was ready to start again. I did some soul searching about what I enjoyed about my past career and assessed my strengths (*this is where the retirement books were very helpful*). I came up with an idea for a great "encore career" for myself. But in order to pursue it I had to go back to school.

    I always enjoyed learning so the decision to return to school was not a problem, but I was a little concerned about my age (*how many 55-year old students do you know?*). How would I fit into a classroom of millennials? I decided to take an online program to make it a bit easier. It was still challenging. I forgot about the massive amount of time it takes to learn a new topic. I had to learn the new technology of a virtual classroom, a new way to interact with my classmates who I couldn't see, hours of reading and now I had to take tests again (*What was I thinking?*).

    It was exciting to think about learning something new and having the time to enjoy the learning experience. When I went to school in the past it was more about finishing and getting a job than the learning itself. I rushed through my first degree. I was living on student loans and the kindness of my family. My only thought was to finish as quickly as possible and make some money. I went from school to full time employment without any break.

My next degree was necessary to move up in the organization. My boss told me I needed a MBA if I was interested in an executive position so I went back to school. At the time I had just moved my family across the country from California to Georgia and left our entire extended family and support structure behind. My daughter was in middle school and I was leading a large program that demanded 60-70-hour work weeks and unending travel. It wasn't the ideal circumstance to go back to school. For two years I attended classes at night and did homework on the weekends, on airplanes or in hotel rooms, wherever and whenever I could. My memory of that time was doing homework early on Saturday and Sunday morning while my daughter slept. Hoping she would sleep long enough for me to get a week's worth of work done before she woke up – the good news was as a teenager she slept until noon. Once again, the learning was more a means to an end; not learning for the sake of learning. No fun at all.

This time I was doing it for a very different reason. I wanted to enjoy and absorb the subject matter. I wanted to spend the time and effort to experience the program and immerse myself in the classes. I didn't even know if I'd ever use it for a second career or merely to enrich my own understanding.

Everything I do now is because I want to do

it, not because I have to do it. That, to me, is the definition of freedom.

At the one-year anniversary of my retirement I began a completely new chapter in my life. I became a student again and started on a path to a new career. It was very exciting as the first class got underway...

However, it wasn't long before I felt some of that hard fought freedom slipping away from me. I began questioning why I wanted to do this. I found the subject matter interesting but it was a bit annoying to be treated like a student again. And then came the tests... I knew in my heart the tests didn't matter. No one except me cared about how I did on them. Once again that competitive person in me raised her ugly head and I had to be the best. So at a time in my life when it just didn't matter, I was stressed out taking tests again. As the program progressed I found a healthy balance and put it back in perspective. The subject matter itself helped me gain greater insight to my own actions and personality.

I spend a lot of time now talking to people about career and life goals and how to decide what direction makes the most sense to them. It always come down to what is the right decision for this moment in time. Throughout your life what you want and what you need changes. From the frantic days when you're starting your adult life, building a career, starting a family, to a different challenge when you may be starting over, in a new phase of life after the family is grown and your needs are different, or you want to create new meaning or seek a new purpose in life; you can always adjust your plans as new opportunities present themselves. It's important to start with who you are today and who you want to be in the future.

I decided my encore career would be "Executive Coaching". I think I was still trying to hold on to a bit of my old self by focusing on the "executive" part but in time I figured out that coaching was what I wanted to do and it didn't matter the subject matter. My past positions involved a lot of identifying, evaluating and developing talent in the organization. I was both a formal and informal mentor to many and was often sought out as an advisor when people were contemplating change in their careers. One of my core strengths is the ability to make connections between what on the surface may seem to be disparate thoughts. My ability to make connections and create new perspectives help people see a more complete picture of what they want and how it aligns with what's important to them. When people are doing what resonates with their core values they're far more productive (*and happy*), so I tried to help people find that in the workplace. I enjoyed the process of helping someone discover what they wanted out of life and helping them figure out how to get there.

Forward Motion

While I was going through the program for my coaching certification I learned more about myself than anything else. In the program you do a lot of peer and practice coaching. That led me to major insights on who I was and what I wanted for myself going forward. The biggest "aha" moment for me while going through the coaching program was that I didn't need to be responsible for anyone else. I realized that every person has the right to make their own decisions and that my input was not necessary, and in some cases detrimental. I had spent my life in authority roles, mother and business leader, and I found I had assumed this meant I was always required to solve everyone else's problems. Through the coaching process I found I could be a great facilitator and let others take responsibility for making their own decisions and finding their own paths.

It was a liberating change. I spent most of my adult life worrying about others and fretting over what would happen to them. Many times I stepped in to "help" without being asked and took away from them the opportunity to learn and grow and feel confident in their own choices. I did it with the best intention but it was misguided. Then I saw a more effective role for me in the future, a way to help that was more beneficial.

So began my "encore career". As I contemplated opening my own coaching practice so many doubts came up. Could I be as effective as a coach as I was as a business leader? Would anyone pay me to be a coach? And if so, why? With the help of my own coach I was able to make sense of it all and recognize the great gift I could bring to others. I discovered this is what I'm meant to do. I know I can help others and make a difference.

With the belief "if I build it, they will come" I opened an office and began my coaching career. It's my decision now when and how much I work and I keep a balance in my life between work and family. I'm hoping that it will be much like starting my first career without all the angst and fear of failure I experienced the first time around. (*If I don't succeed the worst that will happen is I go back to watching NCIS reruns*). I don't have the same urgent need to make money or to make my mark on the world. Now I'm satisfied if I just help a few people get to the place they are meant to be.

At the end of the grieving process I was ready to let go and look forward to the next phase of my life. These are a few key points I took away from the experience:

MANAGE YOUR EXPECTATIONS.

There will be highs and lows throughout the transition and you need to have faith that at some point you will reach a level of acceptance and move toward the new you.

ACCEPT THE LOSS OF WORK FRIENDS.

There will be a few people you will stay close to but embrace the opportunity to create a new network of friends who will help you write the next chapter.

LEARN FOR THE SAKE OF LEARNING.

Be open to new opportunities and new insights. You just might learn a bit about yourself. Curiosity can be a great substitute for passion until you figure out what feels like the real you.

LET GO OF WHO YOU USED TO BE.

As terrifying as it is to let go, the best version of yourself might be the person you will become. As you embark on a new chapter you bring with you all the talents and intelligence and strengths you've acquired over a lifetime. Now you have the opportunity to repackage and repurpose them for even greater impact.

EMBRACE WHO YOU ARE NOW.

Accept that you are moving toward new possibilities and you can decide what future best fits you. Nothing is permanent so let yourself experiment with new experiences. Keep what feels good and let the rest be interesting but temporary detours.

FIND NEW FRIENDS AND INTERESTS.

The best part of a new direction are the opportunities that await you. You can meet new and interesting people and discover hidden talents and interests. Celebrate and enjoy the freedom of being who you were meant to be.

TAKE THE TIME IT TAKES.

Accept that transitioning is a process and will take time for you to sort out. But when you find yourself binge watching your guilty pleasure TV program… it's time to move on.

Forward Motion

Chapter Eight

Finding a New Direction

"The journey is the reward."
Chinese Proverb

So how does all of this help you deal with a major change in your life? Mine was not an easy one, but the process I went through may help others find their ideal future. When you find yourself in the midst of a life altering change it's often hard to take the next step. You might be trying to use old habits and tools to make new decisions and you're not sure why that's not working. There's a better approach.

The process for making changes in your life, both large and small, has been studied by many experts and there are thousands of books and tools and workshops that all claim that their process or tool will be the "one" to allow you to make the changes you desire. I would agree the *process* is pretty simple and the stages of change are well documented. However, what is very simple in theory is very difficult to execute. It's easy to get stalled between intention and action. Talking about change isn't the same thing as implementing change. What is even more difficult is to decide what changes you want to make and then follow through with actions that produce sustained results. Then there's the emotional side of change…understanding how it affects you and the people in your life is just as important to successful change as the action itself.

I often tell my clients our discussions can be the "safe place" where they can explore whatever path they want. I have no vested interest in the changes they desire. My life will not be impacted if they decide they want to move to Greenland and take up ice fishing or travel around the USA as a rodeo clown. I give them a place to dream about it and then think about why it would make them happy. In this process they may discover they can experience the same type of happiness with something that is not as disruptive to their lives (*or maybe not*). My focus is not to judge their dream, but to help them get to the core of what is important to them and how to use that awareness to create a more fulfilling or purposeful life.

There's a belief that people only make change when the pain of not changing becomes too great. The gap between the intention to change and taking action to make a change can be huge. If you're in a comfortable situation, it's hard to get motivated to make a change. Even if it's not an ideal situation, you know what to expect. Fear of the unknown can be so overpowering many people can't get past it. You may be living a life that is satisfactory and predictable but lacks joy and excitement or is just not a reflection of your true self. You may be at a crossroads in your personal or professional life and you must make the choice to stay on the path you're on or take another.

It could be that you are forced to find a new path by circumstances outside your control. Whatever the catalyst, you know it's time to define a new direction. When you focus on the possibilities ahead instead of looking backwards, what you see may be so compelling you won't think twice about letting go.

How do you get started? Working with someone, a professional coach or a trusted advisor, is one way. Having someone to help you think through what you want to achieve and how to make it happen can bring the clarity and support that enables action. People tend to avoid difficult truths. A supportive coach or advisor can encourage you to answer the tough questions and hold yourself accountable for taking action that will lead to a new beginning. This is a place where you create your vision of the future and begin to take actions to fulfill that dreams.

A personal assessment can also be a good first step. The goal of a personal assessment is to develop self-awareness and understanding. It offers a new lens for you to see yourself through.

It can offer a clear, perhaps novel, picture of you to increase awareness and clarity. Assessments can uncover areas of strength and weakness, your motivation to change, and provide a roadmap for individual development. You have to be able to see where you are before you can create a plan to take you to where you want to be. Change can be easier when it's within the natural boundaries of your strengths and talents and is based on a realistic assessment of your assets and personality.

There are many assessments to choose from and they can be administered by a certified coach or practitioner or even taken on your own. There are even several free ones you can access on the Internet (*I've included a few that I like at the end of the book*). An assessment gives you a starting point, an idea of what's important to you, and may lead you to something you want to explore more. They vary in cost and complexity and you can decide which will work best for you, but the goal is to find out what makes you tick. They are all designed to help you better understand how you express yourself in the world; enhancing self-awareness is the goal. Through self-awareness you're in a better position to see in what environments you might thrive or wither. You gain insight into what motivates you to action and what brings you happiness. The objective of this part of the process is to determine what's most important for you to live a fulfilling life. With this knowledge, you can begin to envision the ideal future for yourself.

If it's so simple, why don't we always make the changes we desire? Because change is hard and it's harder still if you don't have ongoing support during the process to keep you focused and accountable to the outcome you seek. The more meaningful a desire is to you; the more commitment it takes to stay with it. There's a principle in social psychology that suggests when a person argues on behalf of a particular position, he or she becomes more committed to it. So just by telling someone - saying it out loud, it's more likely you will make the change. And when you're in uncharted territory, having the right guide can mean the difference between it being an "ordeal' or an "adventure".

This new path is unfamiliar and you will have many opportunities to fall back or fail to move forward. You may question each step and even a minor setback can create major concerns. Every step takes on more significance when the action doesn't produce the outcome you expected. There's a continuous need to reevaluate and reinforce that you're moving in the right direction. During this stage, it's important that you take time to celebrate your small (*and large*) accomplishments along the way. Every time you celebrate an accomplishment, you create momentum, and build confidence that helps you stay the course.

In a major career or life transition you may fear you have left the best of you behind. This is one of the more difficult challenges. For me, getting past the notion I would never be as good as I once was held me back for a long time. I struggled with how to reconcile my success in the past with a less visible, less externally validated existence. In my past career, I was known and respected in the organization and the industry. I was often sought out for my opinion and was considered a leader in my field. Now I was invisible. I went from being an expert to a novice in the blink of an eye. It's human nature to be more comfortable with the things we're good at. It's uncomfortable to be in a learning role again and feeling incompetent. I was in a new place and felt what I had accomplished was not relevant any more. I feared that I would never reach that level of success again…at least not in the way I defined success at that time. I had to come to terms with the fact that my new life would be different and that was okay. Once I was able to get my ego out of the equation I began to appreciate that the future didn't need to replicate the past. My new direction could be just as rewarding and exciting (*but with a lot less stress*). I could still rely on my intelligence, education and experience, I hadn't lost any of that, I just needed to engage it in a different way.

With a coach or trusted partner, you can visualize where you want to go and create the plan that integrates your unique values, talents, experience, and strengths to realize the outcome you desire. What's important is to make the transition in a way that aligns with who you are and how you want to experience life. By tapping into your inherent values and strengths you can create a plan for change that works for you.

The change process is straightforward. The key steps are:

VISUALIZE YOUR IDEAL OUTCOME.

UNDERSTAND WHERE YOU ARE TODAY.

CREATE AN ACTION PLAN THAT MOVES YOU FROM HERE TO THERE.

IDENTIFY AND ENGAGE YOUR SUPPORT NETWORK.

IDENTIFY AND CREATE A STRATEGY FOR DEALING WITH POTENTIAL OBSTACLES.

EXECUTE THE PLAN.

CELEBRATE YOUR SUCCESS.

In the chapters that follow, we'll go deeper into each of these steps and create a path for your ideal outcome.

Forward Motion

Chapter Nine

Visualize Your Ideal Outcome

"Vision without action is a daydream.
Action without vision is a nightmare."
Japanese Proverb

    The first step to your new destination starts with a vision -- a picture of where you want your life to go and who you want to be. It begins with describing in great specificity what you're trying to achieve. It's essential that you're able to create a vivid picture of the desired outcome. Not just a goal or a destination, you want to experience what it will look like and feel like when you get there, where and when it will happen, who will be there with you and how you, and others, will know you have arrived. There's an old advertising slogan that applies here, "If you can see it, you can be it". If you can imagine what it looks like, to experience it and know what it is when you get there, you can create a plan to reach your destination.

    In addition to my journals, I'm in the habit of taking a few minutes every day to write, or think about, ten things I'm grateful for today and ten things I'll be grateful for in the future. In this process, I'm able to be thankful for all the wonderful things I have in my life at this moment in time and visualize what I'll be thankful for in the future. This daily practice is important because it keeps me focused and reminds me what's important to me. It helps guide the hundreds of small decisions that will lead me to the future I envision.

I'm a person who believes in the power of intention. If you're clear about what you want, it will come to you. It may not be immediate, it may not look like what you imagined, or you may need to take some action to make it happen, but I'm convinced it will come. My belief in this is very strong. I've seen it happen too many times to chalk it up to coincidence.

A perfect example is when my daughter was getting married. We had planned a beautiful *outdoor* wedding on April 25, 2015. Both the ceremony and the reception would be outside and we'd be walking from one location to the other, you guessed it...outside. April is often a dry month for North Texas, but this was the year the drought ended and we saw record amounts of rain. For a year before the wedding I wrote in my gratitude journal every single day "I am truly grateful it is sunny and beautiful on Samantha's wedding day." As the day approached, every single weather report showed rain every day up to the 25th and every day after. On the 24th, the night of the rehearsal dinner, as we were leaving for the restaurant, there was a tornado warning in Ft. Worth and we had to take shelter at the hotel until the tornado passed (*not a good omen for the wedding day*). The dinner had to be moved inside and was late getting started. About this time the event coordinator for the hotel asked if we should implement "Plan B" and move the reception from the rooftop terrace to an internal ballroom. It was the pragmatic thing to do but I knew how much it would take away from the beautiful reception we had planned and how disappointed my daughter would be after all the months of planning and the attention to detail we put into it. I decided to have faith in my intentions and believe that the day of the wedding would be "sunny and beautiful" and I told our coordinator to stick with the original plan. On the morning of the wedding, we woke to a spectacular day. The sky was blue, the sun was shining and there was not a cloud in the sky. It stayed that way all through the day and night and the wedding and reception went exactly as we planned. Now you may think I'm crazy to believe that I can change the weather (*and maybe I am*) but this reinforced in me the power of my gratitude journal. This was just one of many intentions that I have seen come to life due to my focus on the outcome I desired. Since then when anyone wants something, they ask me to put it in my gratitude journal. I always say yes, but I ask them to do the same. It's not my focus that makes the change happen, it's theirs. They are being specific and intentional about what they want and that focus is what creates the opportunity for them to make it happen.

As you begin to envision your ideal future, you sometimes need to get into the right frame of mind. To accomplish this, it's helpful to remember who you were at your very best. What was happening? Who was with you? What about the situation made you feel alive? Engaged? Excited? What values and strengths did you bring to the situation? Through this exploration, you can begin to think about your new direction from a positive place – a fulfilling time in your life and what made it so good. It can give you a sense of what's most important to you, the unique attributes you possess, and how you might use that information to create a more enjoyable and meaningful future.

People don't always know what their ideal future looks like. It can leave you feeling confused and blocked - unable to move forward. Through the process that follows, you can begin to form a picture of a future that brings back the experience of when you were at your very best. You can create a vision of what excited you and how that can bring you meaning and happiness today. Being able to recall a time that was fulfilling, exciting and engaging helps you move past any blocks and see what a new future might hold.

So let's get started… For the remainder of the book, I'm going to share several exercises that are designed to walk you through the process I used for myself, and my clients, to help you clarify what you want and how to find your way there. I suggest creating your own journal *(a notebook will work as well)* to capture the information. Each exercise builds upon the prior one and a journal will help maintain the continuity of your thoughts through the process.

The first exercise will help you to put into words what brought you happiness and a sense of fulfillment - what energized you when you were at your absolute best and what made that happen. The answers to these questions will allow you to remember the moments of your life that had significant meaning and allowed you to be the best version of yourself.

Exercise One: Create a Vision of the Future

Consider a point in your life when you felt incredibly energized, proud, alive, involved, and excited about the situation you were engaged in - a real high point. Describe it in detail.

What did you value most about yourself at this time? Skills, abilities, other attributes?

What about the situation itself? What made it so special? Where were you? Who did you share it with?

What do you consider to be the core factor that gives you life today?

If you could bring about a new future in your personal or professional life, what are three things you would wish for?

Using the answers to the questions above consider the following:

What would an ideal situation look like today? What values, strengths, passions, or competencies would it include?

What past experience did you have that was positive and similar? What about it was positive? How did it come to be that way?

How might that apply to your future desires?

Finally, create a picture of your ideal future. It can be in words, in a drawing, in photographs, anything that captures the essence of what you would like your future to be. Provide enough detail to allow you to see it, feel it, and believe it is achievable.

Chapter Ten

Take Action

"It's never too late to be who you might have been."
George Elliot

    I discovered a few things on the way to my new life that are worth mentioning. First, you have to think about what you bring with you as you make the move forward. I found purging things that no longer had relevance to my new direction was very liberating. I consciously changed my "work uniform". I was no longer comfortable in the suits that had defined me in the past. I needed a more casual and comfortable attire for my new business. It was important for me to project on the outside what I felt on the inside. My clothes, my office, even the activities I participate in now are a reflection of the person I have become.
    If you focus on what you want, everything else comes together. You make your intentions known and the universe lines up to help. When I look back at what I said I desired in my journals, it was clear the life I wanted, the one I described in detail, actually came to pass. It wasn't an immediate

thing, it took time, but the intention was there and things began to happen allowing me to follow the dream to where I am today. Even the most trivial of the thoughts can create action.

Journal Entry 1/29/14: "*So my personal belongings were delivered today from the office. Eight boxes after 28 years. I'm not sure what I want to do with them just yet. They represent my past not my future or my present reality. Do I really want them??*"

    When I left work, I boxed up my office and shipped it to my house. It amounted to 8 boxes of books, files, and other memorabilia. When it was delivered, I put it all in the garage because I just wasn't ready to deal with it. I continued to think about what I should do with it all, where I should put it and if I even wanted to keep it. Months went by and I didn't do anything with the boxes except trip over them. As I continued to move in my new direction, I realized there wasn't much in there that was still relevant. Then just when I thought I'd finally go through the boxes, the rain began.

    It was 2015, and as I mentioned earlier, it started to rain in March and didn't stop until June. This incredible amount of rain (*and hail*) created a big hole in the roof over my garage, right over where I had all the boxes stored. Long story short… the boxes were soaked and most everything was ruined. I ultimately threw out 90% of them. What remained was a few items; reminders of the best parts of my career, a few photos, some challenge coins, and a few small mementos of the places I visited and the people I knew. The rest were artifacts of a person that no longer existed. This was one time when procrastination paid off and the work of deciding which parts of my past to keep was done for me. I had expressed my intentions and things happened to help get me where I needed to go.

    The power of intention has been proven over and over again. What you put your focus on is what you ultimately achieve. This can happen with both positive and negative thoughts so beware of how you think about the outcome. Frame it in positive terms, "this is what I want", verses negative, "I don't want…". Careful, or you might just be using all your focus and energy to create more of what you don't want, resulting in more negativity in your life. The mere act of thinking about what you want in a positive way can produce opportunities to make it happen. There are several exercises in the book "The Magic" by Rhonda Byrne, that provide you a glimpse of how powerful this can be.

    Second, as you contemplate your new life, don't be afraid to experiment with different ideas. You don't know what may appeal to you. You can always change your course if it's not working but you can't know until you try. Most people are held back by fear of a negative outcome. Fear can be stronger than your dream and your desire to make it happen. What we want most and what we fear most can sometimes be the same thing. However, the greatest opportunity for growth can come from overcoming that fear. You have to acknowledge it in order to control it. If you are too attached to the outcome, your fear kicks in. Experimenting can change how you view the outcome. It's no longer "do or die", if you view the outcome in a neutral way there's little risk to trying anything new.

When I was a business leader, I would often mentor others in the organization on how to make strategic career choices. My opinion was the path to the top was not a straight line and in fact the larger the spirals you made while moving up, the greater the body of knowledge you obtained. I would even advise them that a step back might be the best thing for their career.

As a senior manager, I was asked to move to a new location in a different organization. However, the position was only a manager level position (*one level down from where I was*) so I was reluctant to take it. My mentor at the time told me that it was important for me to consider this move as it would better position me for long term growth in the company. I trusted my mentor and took the position…and he was right. Within months, I had been promoted back to senior manager and within the next year I was promoted again to a director position (*a level up from where I started*). That happened because I was willing to take a chance to learn more about the organization. By moving around and learning new skills I became a more valuable leader. It ultimately changed the trajectory of my career. This same advice applies as you define a new purpose or direction in your life. More experimentation leads to more opportunities to find new things that interest you and brings you closer to who you really want to be. Experimenting gives you a deeper understanding of not just what is, but what could be. Ask yourself, "what is the good that can come from this experience?"

While you may not yet know what your true passion is, you can substitute curiosity for passion for the near term. Being open to new experiences may illuminate what excites and engages you. Sometimes we find ourselves stuck in how we believe we have to be, doing what we believe we have to do. View new activities as an experiment and they become low risk adventures. If they're not what you thought they would be, you haven't lost anything, you just discovered this path was not the best for you.

I remember when I was in college seeking my engineering degree. I was focused on getting done as quickly as possible. I had bridges to build and money to make and I just needed to get through the program. But the school had other ideas and required I take "electives" (*classes that had nothing to do with engineering*). Being young and inexperienced I suspected it was just some grand conspiracy to get more tuition from me and I was frustrated. Why on earth did I need to learn those things when they had nothing to do with engineering? Well you can guess the answer... they were some of the best classes I ever took because they gave me a new perspective. They opened my mind to new possibilities. It was about learning to think, developing critical questioning skills and exploring areas of the world I wasn't even aware existed. I was able to experiment with new ideas and change the lens I experienced the world through. I found I had an interest in philosophy and Greek mythology and political science. Later in my life I used this knowledge when faced with new situations that required a different way of thinking. A different perspective can help you discover new paths when you're going through a life change as well. Opening yourself up to new ideas can create options you never considered.

    One new idea I had was to join the local Chamber of Commerce. I thought it would be a way to meet some people in my local community. I had lived in the city for almost twelve years, but because of my work had never really engaged in the community. At the first meeting I attended I met some people in need of a facilitator for a focus group they were conducting. I thought "this might be fun". I always liked working with groups and here was a chance to put my new coaching skills to the test. I ended up working with this team to develop a new approach for their leadership development program. I would never have thought to take my new learning in this direction but it was a great opportunity to blend some new skills, coaching and assessments, with some of my prior skills, talent and leadership development. I met a lot of interesting people and had a great time doing something aligned with my new purpose helping people find new paths in life.

I put a lot of emphasis on defining the ultimate goal or outcome you seek. This is important because it's the "north star" that guides your decisions and helps you navigate to an end point bringing you purpose and happiness. I also encourage you to enjoy the journey. Take a few detours, experiment with different ways to reach your final destination and you may just find new people and activities you enjoy. The destination is important but live your life on the way there and every day can be a new adventure.

I don't have a "bucket list" but I do have a pretty long "to-do list". When I think about what I want to do or see, I don't put it in context of "before I die". For many years I put my hopes, dreams and desires in the future. "When I… (Fill in the blank), then I can be happy". My new approach is to do it now, before the moment passes. I urge you to do the same.

Over the past few years, I've had a lot of time to consider how much time I have left on this planet. There were days when I thought "not much" and others when I thought "too much" but in the end most days I just feel grateful for every day I have and try to live it to the fullest. I still make plans for the future (*how else do you get the best airline fares?*) and I love ticking off the items on my "to-do" list as I go. More important, I try to live in the moment. If I see something that interests me, I explore it, I treat it like an experiment and try it out. There's something very powerful about just saying "yes". You meet new people, you discover new interests and sometimes you walk away and say, "well I won't do that again."

Early in my discovery process I decided to learn ballroom dancing. It seemed like a good idea for a couple reasons. First, I thought it would be a great joint activity for my husband and I and secondly, it would prepare us for dancing at our daughter's wedding. We signed up for lessons and began the process of learning to dance in a structured fashion. It's important to note here, we have always enjoyed dancing but it was more "Saturday Night Fever" than "Dancing with the Stars" type dancing. So we both went into it with an expectation that this would be fun, like the old days when we frequented discos and clubs. Unfortunately, that was not to be.

June R. Shrewsbury

The instructor was a bit of a tyrant and made us do the same steps over and over again, increasing our frustration at being inept and uncoordinated with every step. We started to come up with excuses why we couldn't make it to the lessons. It was just not the enjoyable hobby we had hoped. We left the classes with enough skill to do a respectable dance at the wedding and vowing, "we'll never do that again". The point is, every experiment doesn't work out. You find things you enjoy and you find things you don't. Sometime finding out what you don't like is more enlightening.

Appreciate the fact that you bring all of your strengths, talents and experience to every new situation. Just because you're doing something new you haven't lost your intelligence, your skills, your experience or your strengths. You can use them to bring a fresh perspective to any new opportunity. You have to decide what you want and live with the expectation of it coming, but you also have to help it along by taking action to move forward. The universe rewards action.

Exercise Two: Create an action plan

In Exercise One you created a vision of your ideal future. Now it's time to create a plan to move you from where you are today to that point in the future. Think of this plan as a "living document". Over time you may want to come back and revisit it as you learn more about the journey you're on. When you take an action that doesn't create the outcome you're seeking, you might want to revise it. When you experiment with new things, you might want to add a "detour" to your plan or adapt other elements to incorporate this new direction. You may want to adjust the timelines for certain actions or incorporate additional steps along the way. The main point is this is just a starting point. Once you have a good draft of the plan, you'll want to continue to refresh it as your journey unfolds.

IDENTIFY EXACTLY WHAT YOU WANT TO BE DIFFERENT.

You can't change your situation by maintaining the status quo. You have do something different to have a different outcome. Your goal here is to reduce the distance between what you want and your current reality. A good start is listing exactly what would need to change to experience your ideal future. Be specific.

For example, when I was thinking about my future, I knew that it did not include an alarm clock. In my ideal situation, I would never need an alarm clock again. That limited some of the career options I considered (*any that required an early start time*). I also knew that I no longer wanted to travel for my work. I would only travel for enjoyment. Again, this changed the possible opportunities to consider.

You might want to consider, not just *how* things would be different - no commute, no travel, but also *who* would you be spending your time with - more time with family (*or less*), more time with people that share your values or passions? And *where* you might want to be - the beach, the mountains, the city? Think about what your life would look like if you were to wake up tomorrow and be exactly where you wanted to be. How is that different from where you are today?

When you have created a list of the gap between where you are today, and where you want to be in your ideal situation, you can begin to outline the steps it will take to move toward it.

CREATE A SERIES OF SMALL STEPS.
There's a theory in coaching that suggests you have to "go slow to go fast". The belief is that most sustained change comes through continuing, persistent, methodical steps not "giant leaps forward".

Now there are certain personality types out there (*you know who you are*) that are cringing at that thought right now. However, there is evidence to support the idea that consistent progress - small successes - are what keep you moving toward your goal. When you try to move too fast, you may get disillusioned with the rate of success and abandon the plan completely. By creating smaller, more achievable steps, you can celebrate achievement more frequently and build confidence in your ability to reach your goal. You're also able to create more experiments and adjust the plan as you go. With experimentation, you learn before you take more aggressive action in a particular direction.

I often advise clients to take the minimum action they can in a particular new interest to "test the waters" before they dive in. If possible, volunteer somewhere before you commit to a new position, or lease something before you commit to buy it. Anything that lets you try it out before you commit can help you lower the risk associated with your choice and provide more information for you to make the best decisions.

INVENTORY YOUR ASSETS, AVAILABLE RESOURCES, SUPPORT REQUIRED.

Now that you have a good idea of where you want to go and what it's going to take to get there, you can begin to assess what you already have and what you still need. Create an inventory of everything you can rely on as you begin to change your situation.

Start with your personal strengths, experience and connections. At what do you excel? Are you a great speaker or sales person? Are you extremely compassionate or a great leader? Do you have a solid support network, good business connections? What is unique about your skills and experience that may be important to your new future? How could you "repackage" your skills to align with your new interests?

When I decided to pursue coaching, I knew my strengths included good communication skills and being able to think strategically - "see the bigger picture". I use those strengths to better understand what my clients are seeking; effective listening for clues on where they are and where they want to be; helping them articulate what they want; and helping them find a new perspective on their situation, one that may be bigger than they are seeing at the moment. All these are skills I used as a business leader but "repackaged" to use in a coaching scenario.

Next you may want to inventory your tangible property. What do you already have that will move with you to your future? Books? Materials? Tools of the trade? Do you already have the space you need for your new life or can you "repurpose" something to create it?

Finally, who do you have in your life that can provide the support or resources you need but don't have? The next exercise will help you define this more fully, so at this point just think about where your gaps exists and what you would need to close them.

CREATE A DRAFT SCHEDULE OF WHEN ALL THE STEPS SHOULD BE TAKEN.
The final step in creating a plan is to put all the actions together in a time sequence. What actions must happen first, second, third, etc.?

One way to get started is to think about what is the smallest step you can make to start moving forward. Think about what you might already be doing today that you can incorporate into your new direction. Another way to create an action list is to brainstorm all the actions that might be required, in no particular order, and then make the logical connection about what must happen, in what sequence, to make to work. The objective here is to outline everything you will change to make the transition from where you are today to where you want to be tomorrow. The specific actions may evolve over time or you may realize you need some intermediate steps to achieve each action, but you can start with a basic plan and then refresh is as you go.

Chapter Eleven

Build your support network

> *"A friend is one that knows you as you are,*
> *understands where you have been,*
> *accepts what you have become,*
> *and still, gently allows you to grow."*
> William Shakespeare

One of the most important elements when embarking on a new path is creating a strong support network. It can be the difference between making a successful change or not. I define it as all the people in the world that can help you achieve your desired outcome. It can be family, and for those of us lucky enough to have a strong family connection, it starts there, but it is so much more. It's every person that can help you get to where you want to be. It can be family, friends, colleagues, neighbors or past business associates or classmates. Any person that is willing to help you if you ask. It could be people you helped in the past when they were in need or people you just meet along the way. These are the people that are willing to provide you something you need at that moment in time when you most need it. While the journey is yours alone to make, it's better and more fun if you don't have to go it alone.

    A great deal of my business success can be attributed to my support network. When I was still in my corporate role, I couldn't have accomplished what I did without my family. They were my cheering section, my conscience, my therapists, and my friends. When I was uncertain or afraid, they were there, when I experienced the highs and lows of my career, they were there, when I decided it was time to call it quits, they were there, and when I began my new life they were still there. The stability of having them there, being able to count on them, made it easier to make tough decisions. I knew I couldn't fall too far no matter what I decided to do because they would be there with me every step of the way. I could count on them to provide the support I needed, when I needed it. Whether that was helping me make a difficult decision, move across the country or just offering me solace when I was confused or overwhelmed, they were the safety net that gave me the confidence to try new things. People who see the best in you, bring out the best in you, so surround yourself with them. This is what a support network is all about.

    As you create the plan for your ideal future, think about who your support network might be. Include those that are closest to you but also think about other alliances you could form that would enable you to stay on course. People who know more about the designation you seek or the journey you will be taking. The stronger the network -- the greater your potential for success.

You can expand this circle if you think about like-minded people that are passionate about the same things you are. For example, joining a network of people in similar circumstances or with similar interests. When I started coaching I joined the local chapter of the International Coaching Federation (ICF) to meet other coaches and to learn more about the profession I had chosen. It was a place to gain acceptance and get reinforcement for the action I was taking. I met several people that became my extended support network. People I could turn to when I was trying new skills or when I found myself in unfamiliar territory and needed guidance. It was through these relationships I gained confidence to try new methods of coaching and to focus my energy in the areas where my unique talents would be most aligned. They provided a safe place to ask "dumb" questions when I was starting out and helped me through the early days of creating a new business I knew nothing about. They understood I was new at this and provided encouragement and support while developing my new skills.

When you decide to create a new life you impact everyone your life touches. There can even be a tendency to hold back or not vocalize the things you most desire for fear of upsetting those closest to you. The choices you make could have direct or indirect impact on their lives. You could upset their plans and dreams and not even realize it. It can also be as challenging for them to adapt to the "new you" as it is for you. When you can engage their support it's easier to take action, move forward and enjoy the journey.

My husband of 37 years was with me through all the changes I made. He was always supportive, encouraging and understood why it was important that I took the action I did. He looked forward to a time when we had more time together and not so many demands on us. He also understood that it would mean big changes in our lives. While I was lost in my own thoughts, he had changes to deal with as well. Suddenly I was there every day, in his space, changing the way he did things. I disrupted his routine and was not always a pleasant addition while doing it (*my grieving process was not always fun for either of us*). I was taking away what he believed was "his job", what gave him purpose. Small things, like who would do the grocery shopping now, had to be renegotiated. And the larger issues of how we would spend our time together, and just as important, how *much* time we'd spend together, also had to be addressed. We had defined roles and routines for many years and now those were changing. He was forced to adapt along with me as we both moved to a new "normal".

We had just started to settle into the initial adjustments retirement brought when I sprung it on him that I wanted to go back to school and back to work. Many of the plans that we had made were now in flux again. He had to adjust to yet another new direction. His life was disrupted and his plans were changed… again. However, by including my husband in my planning I was able to minimize the disruption to his life and gain his support for the direction I chose. I'm not suggesting that change is not good or necessary, but it helps to be sensitive to the impact it has on those around you.

Early in my career I was asked to relocate from California to Georgia. At the time my daughter was only eleven years old. In California, our extended family was close enough that we saw them all the time and spent every holiday with them. My daughter was very close to her grandparents and her aunts. When we moved, I didn't fully appreciate the "collateral damage" that one decision created. Her grandparents and aunts understood it was necessary for my career, but that didn't make the outcome any easier. It wasn't until much later I even realized how devastating it was to everyone we left behind. I was so caught up in my own career advancement, the impact on them didn't even cross my mind. My only focus was on what was important to my immediate family and me. Many years later when one of my close family members decided to move away from me, I finally understood how it felt and I regret I wasn't more sensitive to the impact it had on my extended family.

Recognize that contemplating or making a big change impacts many others. You may be so absorbed in your own thoughts you fail to see it. And even if you do, you may not know how to deal with it and your own issues simultaneously. This can derail even the best of intentions. With the support of the people in your life you rely on, it's much easier to make a sustainable change.

Exercise Three: Create your support network

This exercise will help you identify all the people in your life that can help as you begin to seek out a new direction.

Draw a series of concentric circles with you as the center.

Label the rings from the inside moving out with the following… family, close friends, business colleagues, past friends and classmates, past business colleagues, neighbors, community affiliations, business groups, other.

In each circle write the names of those people that could provide some type of support to you. It could be something as simple as encouragement, advice, or emotional support, or it could be more tangible such as a social or business connection, necessary resources, or anything else you need to realize your desired outcome.

Think about people that have helped you in the past and those that you helped. It's quite a gift when someone can repay a favor from the past. Think about what you really need and who in these circles can provide it. Be creative and consider at least one thing that each of these people can add to enable your best possible outcome. Think about how you can engage them in a way that is important and valuable to them as well. Maybe they share your passion, maybe they are potential partners, maybe they are just good people that love

Forward Motion

you and want to help you be successful. Use this as a starting point as you begin to move forward and then update it as your adventure unfolds.

Chapter Twelve

Overcoming Obstacles

"When it's obvious that the goals cannot be reached, don't adjust the goals, adjust the action steps."
Confucius

You have a destination in mind and you've outlined a plan to get there and a great support network to assist you along the way. Now your success is inevitable, right? I wish I could say it was that easy, and maybe for a fortunate few it will be the case, but for me it wasn't easy. There were obstacles that got in the way.

The first, and most difficult, obstacle to overcome for me was fear. Fear of the unknown. Fear of a new direction. Fear of becoming "less than" who I was in the past. I was concerned my new life would be small in comparison to the life I left and my value to the world would be underwhelming. I sensed this was the case when I stumbled when introducing myself to new people, people who didn't know what I had accomplished in my prior roles. I found myself unsure of what I had chosen to do with the rest of my life. It wasn't because I didn't enjoy it or that I didn't think it was important, it just didn't feel as significant as what I'd done in the past. I found it difficult to value my services and even more difficult to ask to be compensated for them.

I went back to school, did the work to get the necessary credentials and opened my office. Even with all that completed, I lacked confidence I could be as competent with this profession as I'd been in my past profession. I had a few clients and a lot of good ideas but was struggling to make it more than just an interesting hobby. I knew in my heart this was the right direction for me but my ego was tripping me up. I was getting in my own way. I had to remind myself my new purpose was to live my life doing something I love in a way that created balance in my life. My ego was the only thing holding me back from enjoying what I had created.

Sometimes you have to adjust your attitude to change the situation. Imagine you're lying in bed one night and you hear a trickle of water. At first you think it's a leaky faucet. You start to think about what's causing the leak, and wondering if it's causing any damage to other areas. What's it going to cost to repair it? Are you going to have to take time off to deal with a plumber? And on and on it goes and your anxiety just grows and grows… but then you realize what you're actually listening to is a natural spring that's running outside the bedroom window. What does that do to your stress level? Now the sound is something soothing, meditative and relaxing and may even lull you to sleep. How we perceive a situation, whether it's good or bad, changes how we respond to it. We have control over how we interpret the situation and therefore we can change the outcome. As you consider potential obstacles to your achieving your desired outcome, this approach can be a powerful way to remove them. You can be transported from a difficult ordeal to an effortless joyride.

Your obstacles may seem very practical, like lack of money, or not having the resources or skills you need. But your true limitation is the *belief* that you lack options. By looking at the situation from a new perspective you will see options to get all the support you need. Richard Bach in his book *Illusions – The Adventures of a Reluctant Messiah*, said it well, "If you argue for your limitations then they are yours." Look for alternative ways to find the support you seek. They may be unconventional, they may be difficult, they may require you to try something new, but they exist.

Resilience has been described as the process of adapting well in the face of adversity, trauma, tragedy, or even significant stress. It's what gives you the psychological strength to cope, to handle obstacles and to rebuild after making a significant change. During a major transition everyone experiences varying degrees of setbacks. Some of these challenges might be minor, (a delay or disappointment) while others may feel much more significant (loss of key support or resources). How you choose to deal with the obstacle can play a big role in the outcome. Resilient people are able to utilize their skills and strengths to cope with and recover from setbacks and not dwell on them. Resilience doesn't eliminate stress or difficulties. However, people who possess resilience accept that setbacks happen and that sometimes life is difficult. You may still experience the emotional pain, grief and/or sense of loss that comes after a major change, but being resilient can help you work through it more effectively. It can give you the strength to tackle problems head on, overcome adversity, and move forward.

According to many experts, you can learn how to become more resilient. Here are a few ways to build up your resilience:

SEEK OUT PERSONAL CONNECTIONS.
Maintaining positive relationships with colleagues, family members and friends can build resilience through support from those who care about you. Use the support network you created in Exercise 3 to identify those people in your life. Let them help you work through or around obstacles.

ACKNOWLEDGE NOT EVERYTHING IS AN INSURMOUNTABLE PROBLEM.
Stressful events happen, but you can control how you interpret and respond to them. Plan ahead to avoid crises or develop contingency plans to deal with those that can't be prevented. Be open to the "silver lining" in every situation. Take the time to consider what did go well or what you could be grateful for in a crisis.

ACCEPT CHANGE IS INEVITABLE.
Recognize that there are some goals that will not be achievable in the manner you desire. Be willing to change your perspective and look for new ways to achieve your desired outcomes. You may need to re-think the actions you have developed if they are not getting you to your end goals.

MOVE TOWARD YOUR GOALS.
Recognize that small steps lead to big changes. Set goals that are achievable and make consistent progress. In the words of Chinese philosopher, Lao Tzu, "The journey of a thousand miles begins with one step". Dream big but break it down into the small steps that move you forward. One helpful exercise to overcome stagnation or procrastination is to identify one small but meaningful action you can take today, one week from today, one month from today, and one year from today to move you

toward your goal. It helps you create momentum today while giving you something to work toward in the future.

TAKE ACTION.
Act on adverse situations in areas within your control. Rather than ignoring the issue or hoping that the issue will just go away, think of one action within your control you can take to counter the adverse effects. Create movement to overcome the inertia of doing nothing.

LOOK FOR OPPORTUNITIES FOR SELF-AWARENESS.
Use self-reflection or assessments to understand your strengths, behavioral style, preferences and personality. Use this knowledge to engage your strengths to help the situation. What strength or skill can you employ that can enhance your current situation?

NURTURE A POSITIVE VIEW OF YOURSELF.
Have confidence in your ability to solve problems and trust your instincts. Use the results from Exercise One to illuminate your strengths and where you have been successful in the past.

KEEP THINGS IN PERSPECTIVE.
Even when facing very painful events, try to consider the stressful situation in a broader

context. Maintain a long-term perspective and consider that everything in life is temporary. One trick that works for me is to consider this situation five minutes from now, five days from now and five years from now. You may find that what is painful in the moment may not be very meaningful in the grander scheme of life. It might help you determine what decision is in your long-term best interest.

MAINTAIN A HOPEFUL OUTLOOK.

An optimistic outlook enables you to expect good things will happen in your life. Negative emotions restrict our options. Positive emotions promote growth and discovery. When you're in a positive frame of mind, you are able to see opportunities more clearly and deal more effectively with setbacks.

TAKE CARE OF YOURSELF.

Understand your own needs and feelings. Do what you enjoy and find relaxing. Taking care of you helps to keep your mind and body ready to deal with situations that require resilience.

Identifying and understanding potential obstacles you might encounter as you move toward your ideal future, and being proactive about creating strategies for overcoming them, is a good way to develop resiliency. Each time you're able to overcome an obstacle your confidence grows in your ability to conquer the next one.

Early in my coaching practice, I was having difficulty finding new clients. I wasn't sure how to reach out to prospective clients with a compelling argument for why they might benefit from coaching and why I was the best coach they could use. One of my colleagues suggested I try using a leads service. At first it was exciting as I got several callbacks. However, as the clients came in for their introductory session, I realized that many of them were looking for assistance that I couldn't provide. I ended up sending them to other people that had the niche skills they required. At this point, I felt like giving up. I was not attracting the clientele I thought I could most help. In time my resilience kicked in and I developed a new approach to marketing that better articulated what type of coach I wanted to be and what type of client would most benefit from my unique set of strengths and experiences. Once I was clear on what I had to offer, and was able to better communicate it, I was able to attract the clients I could really help.

Self-efficacy is the strength of your belief in your ability to succeed in a particular situation. It can influence how well you persist when you are not making progress at the pace you intended or when the obstacles feel overwhelming. It can affect your belief regarding your power to affect the situation and can influence how you face challenges as well as the choices you are most likely to make.

As with resilience, you can develop self-efficacy. Here are a few ways increase your self-efficacy:

EXPERIENCE THE SITUATION.
Stop thinking about it, and as Nike says, "Just do it". Start with a small step or goal and experience success. With each success your confidence and your belief in yourself will grow. Imagine one of your role models and how they might accomplish the action you want to take. "See" success achieved and experience it through them.

ENGAGE YOUR SUPPORT NETWORK.
Get someone on your side. Surround yourself with people who appreciate your strengths and will support you in the pursuit of your goals. Everyone can benefit from having a "cheerleader" in his or her corner. When people believe in you, you begin to believe in yourself.

ADOPT A POSITIVE ATTITUDE.
Positive emotions enhance self-efficacy and negative emotions diminish it. Be hopeful and see the positive potential for each situation. Recall past accomplishments and how you used your unique set of skills and experience to create a positive outcome.

ADOPT A GROWTH MINDSET.

Going into a situation seeking only to enhance your learning can free you from the fear of failure. If your only goal is to learn something new, you don't have to worry about the outcome. You simply are increasing your knowledge and adding to your repertoire of skills and experience.

How you approach any major life change can be heavily influenced by your mind-set or the way you experience life. In Carol Dweck's book *"Mindset – The New Psychology of Success"'* she describes two different types of mindsets, "fixed" and "growth" (*she also did a wonderful TED talk that explains this concept that you can find at* www.ted.com/speakers/carol_dweck). In her book she describes the two mindsets and how each influences a person's experience in different situations. She has a simple exercise in her book you can use to determine which mindset you have. She suggests that if you have a fixed mindset, you believe your qualities are carved in stone. No amount of effort can change your core abilities and in fact, effort is for those that lack abilities. Looking smart is most important to you. A setback can be seen as a failure and difficult to recover from. However, if you have a growth mindset, you believe that effort is what ignites ability and turns it into accomplishment. Learning is most important to you. Those with a growth mindset find success in learning and growing. For them setbacks can be motivating and informative. Your mindset also influences how you view failure. If you have a fixed mind set, you see failure as a personal thing, "I am a failure", versus a growth mindset that sees failure as an action "I failed". How you respond to the failure is then impacted by that thought process. The good news is she has also shown that you can consciously change your mindset. Just being aware of which particular mindset you have can begin to influence how you think. As you consider making changes in your life, your mindset can help you or hold you back. Being open to the possibility that each setback is just a learning experience and part of the journey to learning something new, can make it much easier to recover from it.

My motto in life has been "If you think you can, you can. If you think you can't, you're right." So much of what we accomplish in life is determined by our own belief that we can make it happen. When I was growing up in Southern California, my family was poor. I was one of five children being raised by a single mother who herself had only a high school education. She encouraged us all to go to college and get an education so we could have a better life. Unfortunately, it was only going to happen if we did it on our own, there was no "college fund" to help us along. But my mother gave me something more important than money to go to college, she instilled in me the belief that I could do anything I wanted to. With hard work and determination, I could have any life I desired. Even though putting myself through college was difficult, I never doubted I could do it, I never doubted I could find a great job when I graduated, and I never doubted I could have any life I chose. A firm belief that no goal was too far to reach for has allowed me to succeed at anything I put my mind to. This is what self-efficacy is all about, a belief that you have within yourself the skills, abilities and strength to reach your goals whatever they may be.

Exercise Four: Identifying Obstacles

Using the action plan you developed in Exercise three identify the potential obstacles that could derail or delay you in accomplishment of each action.

For each obstacle, think of one action you could take to prevent the obstacle from happening, one action you could take to recover if you are unable to prevent it from happening, and one action you could take to create a new direction if that obstacle can't be removed.

Now go back to your support network and see if there are additional actions you want to add to the support you might want to ask for.

Remember...

> *"If plan "A" didn't work, the alphabet has 25 more letters."*
>
> Unknown

Chapter Thirteen

Make it Stick

*"Work on yourself first,
take responsibility for your own progress."*

I Ching

You have a solid, achievable plan to reach your desired outcome firmly in your grasp. You've created an amazing support network to help you along the way. You've thought about potential obstacles that may be out there and how you'll deal with them. But how will you stay on the path? How will you ensure success?

This is where personal accountability kicks in. You have to make a commitment to yourself that you will take the actions you create and reach out when necessary to avoid those potential boulders in your path. You have to create ways to keep yourself accountable for the promises you make to yourself. When the going gets tough, you need to be able to keep going.

Personal accountability is about being willing to answer for the outcomes resulting from your choices, behaviors and actions. It's also about being honest with yourself and what's important to you. You're choosing to take ownership and responsibility for your life. You're choosing to take action and remove roadblocks (including negative thinking and excuses) and hold yourself accountable for your decisions.

There are several ways to increase your ability to stay the course and reach your goals. By being personally accountable for the outcome you are taking the step of making that commitment. Here are some additional ways you can keep yourself accountable:

BE CLEAR ABOUT THE OUTCOME YOU SEEK.

State your desired outcome in a positive way, "this is what I want" not "this is what I *don't* want". Define your outcome in terms of something that can be self-initiated and self-maintained. You only control your own thoughts and actions. Being clear on what's in your control can help frame the outcome in achievable terms. Identify how you will know, in objective measures, if you have succeeded in your goal.

BE HONEST WITH YOURSELF AND OTHERS.

Accept the reality of what is happening to you whether that's consistent with your expectations or not. If you're honest with yourself, you can better navigate the next actions. You can discontinue unproductive paths and seek new directions when necessary.

DON'T USE BLAME OR EXCUSES WHEN THINGS DON'T WORK OUT.

We all experience setbacks as we take on new activities. You may need additional training or expertise, or the environment isn't suitable, or you simply are not in the right place at the right time. Blaming others (*including "the universe"*) or making excuses for a setback is not productive. It holds you back from seeing or taking other actions that might deliver a better outcome.

FOCUS ON WHAT YOU HAVE CONTROL OVER.

Remember, you only have control over your own actions and beliefs. You can hope or wish that you can control everything, but it won't make it happen. In most instances you have two choices, you can accept the situation as it exists and adapt your own beliefs and behaviors to make it work for you or you can leave the situation. Anything else will just leave you feeling frustrated or blaming someone or something else for your circumstances.

BE WILLING TO ACCEPT RESPONSIBILITY WHEN THINGS DON'T TURN OUT AS EXPECTED.

Sometimes it is your fault. It's not an easy thing to accept, but our decisions don't always produce the outcome we seek and we have to accept the consequences. If your action ends up hurting someone or something the best response is to apologize and make it right.

AVOID PROCRASTINATION.
This is a great way to avoid doing something outside your comfort zone. Take the time to understand why you're putting something off and deal with the underlying issue.

DON'T OVERCOMMIT.
If you can't add something to an already overburdened schedule, you can say "no" and still preserve the relationship if you are honest about how much more you can really take on.

MAKE CHANGES TO YOUR PLAN WHEN NECESSARY.
If something is not producing your desired outcome, try a new approach. There are many different ways to accomplish any task, find the one the works best for you.

Exercise Five: Accountability Actions

    Think about what you can do to hold yourself accountable for the action plan you developed. Focus on what you want to achieve and how important it is to you. What are you willing to do to make it happen? How committed are you to seeing it through to the end? You may want to create an incentive for yourself that you trigger with each small success. You may want to identify an "accountability partner" – someone who shares your passion for making the change happen. You may want to write a daily mantra to keep you on your course. You may want to create an artifact or a physical object that you can see every day that reminds you of the person you really want to be. Think about what has worked for you in the past to maintain your focus. Create a tangible reminder that will keep you accountable for making the changes you desire.

    I had a mantra that I repeated every day to myself, it was "Every day, in every way, I'm getting stronger and stronger, healthier and healthier, happier and happier." I would say this to myself while I was walking or riding my bike or just relaxing on the couch. It was a reminder to myself to continue to focus on what was important to me, being strong, healthy and happy.

    In your journal (*or notebook*), you have created the beginning for your journey. You've visualized

Forward Motion

the best possible future for yourself. You've created a plan for closing the distance between where you are today and where you want to be in that future. You've identified the people in your life that can help you travel to this new place. You've thought about what might get in the way of your destination and how you can effectively deal with it and keep moving forward. You've made a commitment to yourself to hold yourself accountable for making it happen. This is a great time to take a moment and celebrate that you took the first step toward creating a life that brings you meaning and happiness.

Chapter Fourteen

The Journey Continues

"The mystery of human existence lies not only in just staying alive but in finding something to live for."

Fyodor Dostoyevsky

You have reached your goal, you're living the life you have imagined and you're comfortable with the place you find yourself. Take time to celebrate! So often we work very hard to reach a particular goal only to see the moment come and go without the fanfare it deserves. There will always be new mountains to conquer and new opportunities to undertake but don't lose sight of what you have already done. Being able to appreciate the results from your efforts underscores your ability to make decisive change in your life. Use this success to propel you to your next adventure.

When I completed my coaching certificate and received my ICF certification I felt an enormous relief. I had the "credentials" I needed for my new life. What I failed to recognize was I had been coaching and helping people all along the way. The credentials were nice (*and necessary in some situations*) but they did not make me a coach. What made me a coach was the fact I was engaged in living the life I designed. I was using my unique set of talents and skills to help others on their journey to make changes they desired in their own lives. The credential marked the event for me and gave me a milestone to celebrate.

    This story is about learning to let go of the past and embrace new beginnings. My new life is more authentic and more enriching than the one I used to have. While my old life had exciting adventures and was fulfilling at times, what I want, and need, at this point of my life is different. I suspect that in the next 10 to 20 years my desires will continue to change. And as those new directions unfold, I'll revisit this process to say good-bye to the old and accept the new. I know there are many more adventures out there for me. With each new experience I find an opportunity to expand my life and find joy in new activities, with new friends and colleagues.

    In the process of writing this book, my life continued to evolve. In addition to coaching, I found myself facilitating teams and groups, working with organizations on leadership development programs and consulting with small businesses on how to better develop and market their unique product offerings. The most

June R. Shrewsbury

exciting development was joining with my sisters to create a publishing company for a series of children's books focused on helping parents create opportunities for their children to live healthier, happier lives.

These may seem like unrelated activities, but they all stem from a common value of wanting to help people make the most of their lives. Even though I defined my "north star" and had an action plan to get there, I kept my mind open to all the different possibilities presenting themselves along the way. My curiosity allowed me to explore them, through experimentation I was able to "try them on" and when something aligned with my core values, I was able to find ways to incorporate it into my new life. Your experience will be different but may encompass many of the same elements.

Life is a series of transitions, some small, some life changing, but each one is a new beginning. A new opportunity to experience life to its fullest. We can reinvent ourselves as often as we please; it just takes a little focus, action and support. How many new lives can we have?... as many as we like.

"Go confidently in the direction of your dreams.
Live the life you have imagined".
                                    Henry David Thoreau

Forward Motion

Additional Resources

Meyers Briggs Type Inventory – Four dimensions of personal style and preferences. www.myersbriggs.org

Clifton Strengths Finder – Identifies your top 5 strengths out of 34 possible. Enables you to generate an action plan online. www.gallupstrengthscenter.com

VIA (Values in Action) Signature Strengths – no cost assessment based on Positive Psychology and a value-based approach to strengths. www.authentichappiness.com

Various Assessments – Allows you to assess multiple dimensions of your personality. www.psychologytoday.com/tests

Forward Motion

References

Byrne, R. 2012, *The Magic*, New York, Atria Books

Cooperrider D. and Whitney D. 2005 *Appreciative Inquiry: A Positive Revolution in Change*, San Francisco, CA, Berrett-Koehler Publishers

Dweck, Carol S. 2006, *Mindset – The New Psychology of Success*, New York, Random House

Hagerty, B. 2016, *Life Reimagined: The Science, Art and Opportunity of Midlife*, New York, Riverhead Books

Kubler-Ross, E. and Kessler, D. 2005, *On Grief and Grieving: Finding the Meaning of Grief Through the Five Stages of Loss*, New York, SCRIBNER

Forward Motion

To learn more about the author or to get additional insight and resources for the process that June Shrewsbury outlines in this book, visit her at www.jrshrewsbury.com

Forward Motion